Glimpses of Gayton

Glimpses of Gayton

A pictorial history of a Northamptonshire village

Rita Poxon

Sue Clayton

Published in 2000 by

Sue Clayton
Japonica House, Flintham
Newark, Nottinghamshire NG23 5LA

© Rita Poxon, MA

ISBN 0 9533350 1 1

Designed by *Trevor Clayton*

Printed in Great Britain by
Technical Print Services Ltd
Brentcliffe Avenue, Carlton Road, Nottingham NG3 7AG

Contents

Front and back cover photographs by

Rod Poxon, LRPS

Acknowledgements

Following an initial suggestion by Betty East many people have participated in the preparation of this book, making it a true community project. But first, on behalf of everyone, I must thank the Millennium Festival for making a large award to Gayton from the Heritage Lottery Fund, as well as South Northamptonshire Council and Gayton Parish Council. Their funding has enabled the original idea to be realised.

The project was designed not only to create a pictorial history book but also to produce a large archive of photographs of Gayton over the years to be deposited in Northamptonshire Record Office. Rod Poxon has painstakingly copy photographed every single picture submitted and meticulously kept an index of all the information provided. As the photographs put forward were well over twice the number anticipated his workload far exceeded expectations. However, as a consequence, Gayton now has an unprecedented record of its past for future generations to admire, stored locally as well as at the Northamptonshire Record Office, and many will be available on CD.

The photographs have been provided from family albums and attics around the village and beyond. Without so many to choose from we would have been unable to illustrate life over the years so fully. Thanks go to Cyril Hillyer, John Gilkes, Colin and Jenny Wakelin, Joan Adams, Walt Newcomb, Bill Nightingale, Audrey Smith, Jackie Huckerby, Margaret Shepherd, Wendy Briglin, Chris Wilcox, Norman Robinson, Mervyn Cockerill, Tony Rogers, George Freeston, Roger East, Elizabeth Neale, Hazel Cohen, Pete Butcher, Anne Warren, Brenda Nightingale, Bob Mansfield, Joan Chester, Wendy Steer, Connie Reid, Betty and Michael East, Viv Huckerby, Pearl Etherington, Joan Wreford, Chris Rankin, Ken Cokayne, Janet Wilkins, Johnny Gordon, the *Chronicle and Echo (Northampton),* Peter and Julie James, Melissa Hunt, James Price, Rene Dundas, Margaret and Tony Ratledge, Roger Warwick, Peter Pettifer, Gareth Poxon, Rita and Rod Poxon, Gayton Parochial Church Council, Sidney Sussex College and Northamptonshire Record Office for photographs included in the book. In addition Ros Agar, Pam Clayton, Barbara Ratledge, Margaret Lattimer, Betty Hammersley, Eric White, Angela O'Dwyer, Brian Pawley, Mary Watterson, Jim and Carol Hollin, Deryck Blunt, Anna Fox, Margaret McLain, Alison Huckle, Evelyn Eales, Hilda Billing, Sam Cokayne, Ted Gould, Barbara Bryan, Eunice Brownlee, Pat and Rita Morrison, Stuart Woolston, B King, Jonathan and Penny Taylor, Pat Taylor, Viv Hartley and the National Monuments Register, have all provided other documents, information, anecdotes and photographs which have enhanced the project. I would also like to remember Nancy Paul and Nobby George who spent many hours talking to me about Gayton.

I would particularly like to express my gratitude to those who helped with my research. Hilda Billing provided quality control. Tony Rogers has spent hours identifying people in the photographs with the help of older residents. Peter Pettifer has frequently visited the Lincolnshire Archives Office referring to the Hawley papers kept there and Lorraine King visited Maidstone Record Office, also on the trail of the Hawleys. Chris Rankin has donated aerial photographs from the National Monuments Register at Swindon. Other Gayton records have been verified at Buckinghamshire, Norfolk, Nottinghamshire and Berkshire Record Offices. I have had help from Northamptonshire Heritage and Northampton Archaeological Unit. Rachel Watson, Crispin Powell and the rest of the staff at the Northamptonshire Record Office have tolerated my questions over many years with patience, and Dr Paul Barnwell at RCHME York has been most kind. Nicholas Rogers, the archivist at Sidney Sussex College, has given me support for a long time, for which I am indebted.

The Lottery Award enabled me to engage the services of a copy editor. Sue Clayton's advice has far exceeded that of purely a copy editor and, combined with the design skills of her husband Trevor, they have contributed a professionalism to our project which has given us a book to be proud of. Nevertheless, any mistakes which may remain in this book are my own.

And finally my thanks go to the other committee members of the Gayton Millennium Project, Gary Keal, Wendy Steer, Tony Rogers, Peter Foster, Pat Morrison and Rod Poxon, who have worked hard to enable our small village to start a new millennium on such a high note.

Rita Poxon
Gayton, June 2000

Glimpses of Gayton

Northampton

GAYTON

Scale

0   5   10 miles

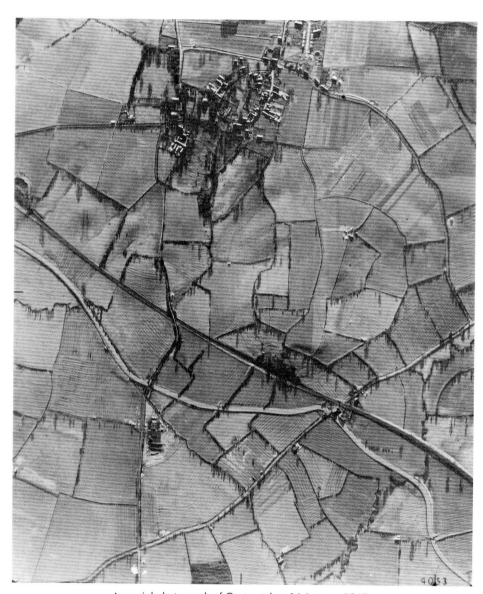

An aerial photograph of Gayton taken 16 January 1947
Crown Copyright/MOD

A Long Time Ago

First signs of life in Gayton

The Early Bronze Age Beaker people

Just think! A group of people lived in Gayton in 1800 BC - that is 3,800 years ago. We know this, because a burial pot, shaped like a beaker, was found in a clay pit on Gayton's border with Milton Malsor and Rothersthorpe. The beaker, or cinerary urn, contained the remains of a young girl about 18 years old. So, it would seem that an Early Bronze Age family lived here.

A Roman villa

The next sign of people living in Gayton was nearly 2000 years later between 43-409AD. The site of a Roman villa was discovered in 1840 when ploughing organised by Dr Butler, the Rector, turned up large pieces of masonry. In 1991, when the new A43 was constructed close to the site of the villa, more signs of Roman occupation were unearthed. The most important discovery was a corn drier confirming that people did indeed live in Gayton rather than visit to worship. So, Gayton was inhabited in Roman times although the people were probably well-to-do Britons accepting Roman ways rather than Romans from Italy or some other part of the Roman Empire.

Bronze dancing cupid found at the villa

Roman corn drier discovered during the construction of the new A43 in 1991

A dangerous place to be!

Whether the local story that tells of Danes killed in battle and being buried in mounds on Nine Tree Hill has any justification we may never know. However, this field on the righthand side of Wright's Lane had nine elm trees standing on the top of a large mound. Prior to the Battle of Hastings, Gayton was part of the area controlled by Tosti, the Saxon Earl of Northumbia and brother of King Harold. South Northamptonshire became the battle ground for the Danes holding Northampton and the north of England, and the Saxons who held Towcester and England to the south. Gayton was on the front line. Its position on the top of a hill overlooking Northampton was crucial for the Saxons. The continual threat of invaders must have severely discouraged a high profile settlement. But Gayton seems to have avoided the devastating Northamptonshire battle between Earl Morcar and Harold Godwinson in 1060 which destroyed most of the region.

The triangular doorway shows that a church existed in Saxon times. The bellringers trained so that they could ring in the Millennium in the New Year 2000.

Left to right:
bellringers, George Green, Henry Taylor, Chris Bulleid, Rosie Bulleid, Stan Watterson and Catherine Hartley

The Domesday Book

The Domesday survey of 1086

William the Conqueror won the Battle of Hastings in 1066. He had conquered England and immediately set about discovering how wealthy his new kingdom had made him. The Domesday Book was the result of a survey of landholding and resources. Although Gayton manor is not mentioned by name there is little doubt that it is the unnamed manor held by Sigar de Chocques, who came from a village in the Pas de Calais. He held land from King William in Bedfordshire, Gloucestershire and Hertfordshire but only the village of Gayton in Northamptonshire. However Gunfrid de Chocques, perhaps his brother, held Rothersthorpe and Roade nearby.

How big was Gayton?

Gayton was considered to have land for ten ploughs and valued at £6 for taxation purposes. It contained four hides and four parts of half a hide of land. A quarter of this land, perhaps 120 acres, was in the manor's home farm. The manor employed three ploughs, five slaves and three female slaves. A 'plough' was not only a piece of machinery but considered to be a team of oxen as well. One 'plough' was the land one plough pulled by eight oxen could work in one day. That would vary from place to place as some land was easier to work. Slaves worked for the lord - they owned no land and had few rights.

Within the community there were 21 villeins (villagers who owned land), a priest and 11 bordars who were small holders. These people worked eight ploughs. Also there were eight acres of meadow land, which probably bordered streams, and were used for hay and grazing, and a sixth of a square mile of woodland.

Life in the twelfth century

The Saxons named Gayton

Gayton was named as a manor sometime between 1086 and 1154. Other villages with the same name across the country are thought to be from the Old Norse *geit(a)-tun,* goat's farm. However we know from Domesday that Gayton was the Saxon Earl Tosti's land so it is likely that it developed from a personal Old English name *Gaega.* Perhaps this was the name of the man Earl Tosti put in charge. The Old English ending 'tun' came to mean hamlet or village.

Robert of Bethune gave money to Delapre Abbey

Robert of Bethune, a barrister from Arras in northern France, granted an annual pension from the benefice (church living) of Gayton to the abbess and nuns of the Cluniac nunnery, Delapre Abbey. He probably also endowed Gayton church with land some time before 1234 and recommended William de Albiniaco as the clergyman, on 25 January 1235. From the lords of Bethune, the manor and advowson (the right to put forward a priest) passed to Robert de Guisnes in 1246 and then to Ingelram de Fiennes three years later.

A twelfth-century cooking pot in calcite grit was found by Bob Price on the site of Kiln Yard near Park Lane

Ingelram de Fiennes had permission from the king to create a deer park in 1258. This circular hedge which enclosed 25 hectares at the end of Park Lane is still visible from the manor-house.

3

Michael de Northampton

Michael, the son of Simon de Houghton de Northampton was lord of the manor when he was granted a 'free warren' by the king. The rabbit meat from the warren and venison from the deer park, already allowed to Ingelram, were prized additions to the manor's table.

Juliana and Philip de Gayton

Michael's grandsons died childless. His granddaughter, Juliana, married a local man, and their son Philip inherited the manor. He had the right to appoint the rector and so William de Gayton, a relative of Philip, became acolyte (assistant) and then parson of Gayton.

Military service

Philip was so rich, his income was over £20 per year, that he was required to do military service in person, 'with horse and arms beyond the seas'. In the event he was excused, due to his appointment as Northamptonshire and Warwickshire's representative hearing cases which contravened the Magna Carta and Carta de Foresta charters.

Sir Philip de Gayton died in 1316, five years after his pilgrimage to Compostella. His oak effigy is to the left of the altar in St Mary the Virgin Church, Gayton.

Philip the pilgrim

Philip undertook a pilgrimage to the shrine of St James at Santiago de Compostella in northern Spain which was the third most holy city in Christendom, after Jerusalem and Rome. On 16 April 1311, he received Edward II's licence to travel and letters to carry for his protection. The traditional way to make the journey was on a white horse. Pilgrims carried a scallop shell which could be used as a dish or spoon when eating from the communal stews served to pilgrims at the various hospices along the way. The Cluniac monasteries had popularised the pilgrimage to Compostella and a monk, Aymery Picaud had written a book in 1139 called the *Codex Calixtinus*. This was a tourist guide for pilgrims telling the story of St James before describing the churches and shrines along the route, even the countryside and people.

Confusion followed Philip's death

Philip had three children but his only son, Theobald, died a few days after he did. Philip's two daughters were married. Scholastica who was 24 years old had married Thomas de Meaux and Juliana, the elder was 26 years old and married to Thomas de Murdak. Juliana's friend, Sir John de Vaux encouraged her to plot with him to murder her husband, Sir Thomas de Murdak, hoping to marry her himself and become the lord of the manor she would inherit.

Who killed Sir Thomas de Murdak?

The crime

During Easter week, 1316, Thomas de Murdak was found dead at Edgecote in a most unpleasant way. 'His body had been cut through the middle, his head cut off, and his body dismembered in quarters.' It was alleged that Thomas had been killed in Kinver Forest at Stourton, Northamptonshire by Sir John de Vaux and his brother Ellis, his wife Juliana, her chamberlain Roger, Robert Sumpter, John de Vaus, Robert Purdhome, John fitz Gillian, (his steward and cook), Adam Boffard, Thomas le Taillour, Maud, Mabel of Blayworth and Mabel the wife of Hugh the clerk of Hochecote.

A confession

A Yelvertoft man confessed to having helped the murderers. He claimed that Thomas de Murdak's steward had hit Thomas on the head with a staff whilst he was in bed at Stourton castle. When Thomas tried to get up, Robert, Thomas' chaplain, had thrust a bidewe into him up to the hilt. Roger, Juliana's chamberlain, had then cut Thomas' stomach open with a knife.

Was Juliana burned at the stake?

By the time the king's men arrived all the accused had run away except for Juliana. She was the only one tried for the crime and she was found guilty. Contemporary reports conflict; one says that she was burned to death and another that she was hung. Whatever her fate, the fight through the courts for possession of Gayton manor went on for many years. This was due to an ancient law which allowed the king the profits of Juliana's share of the manor for a year and a day. These profits totalled ten marks (one mark was worth approximately 65p), corn from the farm and fish from the fishponds. Traces of two rectangular fishponds can still be distinguished in a field called Springs Orchard, near the manor-house. Eventually the manor and advowson were sold to Sir William Trussell of Flore in about 1329, but several others held part shares.

Scholastica survives the Black Death

Scholastica, Philip's second daughter, had a grant of free warren confirmed in 1330 and she lived in the manor-house until her death in 1354. Scholastica saw one of the most devastating events in English history, the Black Death. The plague epidemic swept across England in 1348-9, hitting a country whose rising population, weakened by bad harvests, was struggling to produce enough food. In two and a half years, one third of the population died a horrifying and repulsive death. Those that survived were stunned by the swift destruction of their family and friends, and were traumatized by the manner of their death. Scholastica's son, Sir John de Meaux, inherited her share of the manor and on his death in 1377 the Trussell family came into full possession of the entire manor of Gayton.

A Park called La Hay

Theobald Trussell left the manor to his son and daughter-in-law, John and Margaret. In 1404 John was given permission to make 300 acres of land into a park called La Hay, in Gayton. Whether this land extended beyond the earlier park is unclear. Margaret outlived her husband but on her death in 1445 she was buried on the west side of the church and the manor reverted to James Sweetenham. From him it passed to Robert Tanfield and it was to stay in his family for many years.

Is Robert Tanfield's tomb next to the altar?

It seems very likely that the grand tomb next to the altar in Gayton church is that of Robert Tanfield. Although the brass plate has been removed from the back of the tomb, the imprint left follows a pattern common in the sixteenth century for those who had been married twice. Robert Tanfield was married twice. The tomb, being next to the altar implies high status. Robert was a very rich man. In 1471, ten years before he died, Tanfield installed as Rector of Gayton, Thomas Tanfield, a relative who was a doctor of divinity. Robert's son William and his wife Elizabeth, and then his grandson Francis, lived at Gayton Manor. Francis had married Bridget, daughter of Richard Cave of Stanford.

Francis, Bridget and their 18 children

The Manor-house

Francis Tanfield built a cross-shaped house

Francis was well off enough to build a new house for himself, his wife Bridget, and their large family, in 1545, to the north of the church. It is special as there are very few manor houses in the shape of a cross still standing in England. In the north chapel of the church, the incised slab on their monument shows Francis and Bridget in elegant outfits with their 18 children. The eight children who died as babies are represented in swaddling clothes, but one was forgotten and added later. The others are dressed according to their status and sex.

A secret passage?

A mystery surrounds an underground passageway that leads from the manor to the church. Why was it constructed? One theory is that during the Reformation, when England was changing from being Roman Catholic to Protestant and Roman Catholics were persecuted, that a tunnel would allow them to escape arrest. If this is true the connection between the manor in Gayton and the Roman Catholic Tresham family may be the clue. Sir Thomas Tresham held a mortgage on Gayton manor. He was bankrupted by fines for attending Roman Catholic mass and in 1587 he forfeited his lands in Gayton. In addition the Tanfields had close ties with the Tresham Family. Francis Tanfield's daughter, Margaret was married to Maurice Tresham. When Elizabeth I came to the throne in 1558 she acted swiftly to reintroduce Protestantism. Images were removed from churches and an English-language prayer book was made compulsory. Those whose loyalty was uncertain signed the Act of Uniformity quickly to ensure their future prosperity under the new monarch. Interestingly, Sir Francis Tanfield was one of those who signed. Throughout the sixteenth century, members of well known Roman Catholic families such as Catesby, Campion and Vachell lived in Gayton. Sir Francis' grandson, Francis sold the manor in 1607 to the Samwell family.

Moulding for a doorway inside the manor with Francis and Bridget's initials, FᴛB

This is the oldest photograph of the manor-house. The wall around Spring Orchard is higher than it is today.

Sir William Samwell

The Samwells were an old county family. Under their tight supervision, they provided conscientious lords of the manor, when only approved businesses, such as Gayton's oldest inn the Squirrel, could flourish and prosper. Life for the villagers was inevitably made more restrictive when Thomas Samwell, an active magistrate, was the lord. At the same time the Rector, William Gibbs, was vigorously pursuing church matters, the landlord of the inn, Thomas Wilson, was the high constable of Northamptonshire, and a yeoman of the village was the parish constable. Employment for the people revolved around the manor, working on the land, in the manor house or in dependent services.

From 'County' to fishmonger

Thomas Samwell sold Gayton manor to Richard Kent in 1751. Kent made his money as a fishmonger at St Clement Dane in London and considered Gayton manor as an investment. Kent rented the manor to William Payne who farmed the manor farm. According to a local man, George Tymms of Hartpole, Kent actually lived in 'a neat small house' (the fore-runner of Gayton House) when he resided at Gayton. He died within two years of making his investment and his wife, Sarah, within five. Both were buried in Gayton church. In Tymms' opinion, Kent had been unfortunate not to have lived long enough to pay off the mortgage.

Richard Kent junior was an adventurer

Richard Kent junior inherited the mortgage. He was commander of the *Volunteer*, a private ship of war. Tymms disliked Kent's connection with trade and foresaw his financial collapse. James Hawley was looking for an estate and Tymms advised him that one in Gayton was likely to be on the market soon. He reported that the manor was 'an old but seemingly strong stone building' and 'the situation of ye great House is very delightful'. As Tymms foresaw, Richard Kent junior had to put the estate into the hands of trustees for them to sell, as necessary, to pay his creditors. James Hawley MD took over most of the land whilst Kent struggled to retain the property. Eventually Kent was forced to sell the manor in 1755. When the Northamptonshire Militia was formed on 1 March 1763 with ten companies, each of 60 men, Richard Kent was made Captain in charge of one of the companies. Later he became a Major. Richard Kent died in 1780 and was buried with his father and mother in the church. The house his father had lived in, the forerunner of Gayton House, with some land attached, was sold to John Darker.

Dr James Hawley

In 1762 Dr James Hawley had gates and fences put up to separate Gayton from its neighbours. The fences were across the Banbury Lane where it meets the parishes of Rothersthorpe and Pattishall, and across Mill Lane (Eastcote Road) at the parish boundary with Tiffield. These barriers were vandalised. Dr Hawley put up a reward of five guineas to catch 'the Parcel of profligate, spiteful and mean-spirited Fellows; who pretend that this low-liv'd Action is justifiable'. Hawley sold the advowson in 1765 for £1,400 to Sidney Sussex College, Cambridge but retained his interest in the manor.

Sir Henry Hawley

In 1795 the Baronetcy was created by George III. Sir Henry Hawley gradually increased his holdings in Gayton buying when land came on the market. In 1795 the sluice gate of a pond in Gayton Wood was broken, releasing the water and the stranded fish were stolen. As the pond was close to Blisworth and Tiffield, it is not at all certain that the thieves were from Gayton.

Sir Joseph Hawley

Sir Joseph Hawley inherited land in Gayton in the mid 1800s which was suitable for brickmaking and ironstone mining. This industrialisation increased the profit from the land for nearly 100 years. It then returned to agricultural use. The manor passed from Sir Joseph to Sir Henry James, then to Sir Henry Cusack Wingfield and in the 1930s to Sir David Hawley's ownership.

David Hawley, POW

By the early 1920s ironstone mining had come to an end. During the second world war, however, a shortage of iron for armaments led to the re-opening of mines. One of the great local ironies was that permission to re-open the Gayton mines was not forthcoming as Sir David Hawley, now the land owner, was a prisoner of war in Germany! Throughout the war his mother lived at the manor in Gayton but when Sir David returned in 1946 she moved out and the manor was rented to Mr Leslie Church and his wife.

Peggy Hawley

The Hawley family remain major landowners in Gayton, today. As part of Gayton's Millennium celebrations, Peggy Hawley gave a plot of half an acre to the parish for the provision of a Millennium Spinney. The village turned out to plant the trees on 4 December 1999.

Mrs Hawley was the last member of the family to live in Gayton

Planting Gayton's Millennium Spinney on 4 December 1999

Comings and Goings

'Des res' for early settlers

Gayton was a pleasing place to make a home. It had a fine supply of drinking water, a strategic site overlooking the surrounding area, good soil, a supply of wood and stone and it was close to ancient trading routes.

Drinking water in the wells

Despite being situated at the top of a steep hill, there has always been a constant flow of pure underground running water to supply Gayton's many wells. Churnwell Spring rises on the Eastcote side of the parish and follows a course beneath the village centre emerging behind Park Lane. It then continues above ground running down to the water treatment works. Building may have changed the water course slightly over the years as there is a field called Springs Orchard, to the east of today's stream.

The medieval fishpond at Brittains Corner

The case of the disappearing sheep

Many wells still exist in gardens, and even inside houses. A story is told of a well in a field at Fiveways that was filled in and forgotten until three rams, kept in the field 'disappeared'. The underground stream had washed away the rocks and soil fill and the animals were discovered at the bottom of the shaft. In 1992 this episode was nearly repeated when the ground gave way beneath someone's feet in High Street revealing another forgotten well.

From stand pipe to piped water

At the turn of the twentieth century, before the homes of Gayton had piped water, John Hillyer was caretaker of the windmill at the waterworks. He made sure that water was pumped up from Churnwell Spring each day to a reservoir near the village green. This fed the stand pipes around the village. In January 1906 a gale destroyed the windmill causing an interruption to the supply and meant expensive repairs. In case the windmill was damaged again a motor generator was installed but only as a backup measure. On 8 January 1957 the village lost its source of spring water and it was replaced by processed 'clean' water provided by the Water Board. The new taste of chlorine was disliked intensely. The water had declined in standard and villagers complained bitterly about the low quality due to the pipes, and about the water supply being cut off frequently without notice.

Fun skating on the ponds

Louisa Butler wrote of skating in her childhood in the 1850s on Mrs West's pond (at Gayton Wood Farm) and at the Alms House pond (also known as Brittains or Arbutt's pond). She particularly remembered Revd Butler teaching her younger brothers as soon as their ankles could bear the weight of the skates. Dr Butler's son, Revd Dr Henry Montague Butler was reported c1910 as having been one of the finest skaters of his time! When the stream feeding Brittains fishpond was cut off during ironstone mining, the pond became stagnant and in August 1972 was filled in with stone from the newly demolished Gayton House.

Ancient trading routes nearby

Jurassic Way or Banbury Lane?

Gayton, high on a hill, overlooks the Banbury Lane which runs around the north west parish boundary. It was an old drovers' road which allowed cattle to be brought from the hills of Wales to be sold in the cattle markets of Banbury and Northampton, and so on to London. In 1154 Northampton ranked the fourth most wealthy of all provincial towns in England. Through Gayton, the Banbury Lane follows the line of the Jurassic Way. This was a prehistoric track-way, stretching from Gloucestershire to Lincolnshire, and connecting the Iron Age fort at Hunsbury to the Rollwright Stones in Oxfordshire. From its vantage point Gayton has always been well positioned to trade.

Writing letters improved the roads!

The need for better roads became clear when, with more people able to read and write, the postal service evolved. Turnpike Trusts were formed to raise the money to build good roads. Watling Street (A5), the old Roman road, was the first to be improved in Northamptonshire in 1706. Gayton was now only one hour's walk from the posting houses of Fosters Booth. Another main road, Towcester to Cotton End (the old A43), became a turnpike in 1794. This brought the country's important lines of communication even closer to Gayton. Gayton continued to be easily accessible with the building of the M1 motorway in 1959, which is visible from Gayton, and the new A43 in 1991.

Overseers of the Highway

Until 1555 the lord of the manor had to keep the roads in good order but then the responsibility passed to the parish. At the meeting of the Rector and Vestry (any villager who was a ratepayer in the parish could attend) two people were appointed each year to be

Many of Gayton's roads before the motor car must have looked as Goggs Lane does today

overseers of the highways. They levied a tax on villagers for repairing and enlarging roads. In the nineteenth century this responsibility rested on the shoulders of the farmers. Men such as William George, William Griffiths, William Payne, James Payne and William George all took their turn between 1803 and 1812. Today this is the responsibility of the County Council.

Dr Butler changed the road layout
Until 1854 the route to Milton Malsor did not pass between the Manor-house and church, but went in front of the church, around the old Rectory (Wendover) and churchyard, rejoining today's Milton Road at the junction with Wright's Lane. This change kept traffic away from the Rectory, Dr Butler's home, but also gave easier access to a newly created brick works.

Public transport
Public transport grew with the introduction of better roads at the end of the eighteenth century and coaches travelled from one town to another as fast as possible. Village people found it difficult to come to terms with the speed of the traffic. John Cockerill, a butcher and maltster from Gayton, was killed on 2 December 1802 by the wagon tilt of the stagecoach in a narrow passage between the foot of the bridge and the Cocks Head public house, when he was returning from Northampton market. On 14 July 1804 the driver of the Nottingham coach was fined 40 shillings and imprisoned for three months for striking Mrs Rolfe from Rensbury, with his whip when she was returning on her horse from Northampton market. Road rage may not after all be a new phenomenon! Mrs Rolfe was thrown from her horse, breaking both of her legs.

Brittains Corner was straightened and made safer in 1956

Hillcrest Road c1955

Steam engine used to tar Brittains Hill in 1956

Dr King's car before 1920

Single decker service passing Brittains Cottages c1946

Arthur Roberts' first bus was a new Thorneycroft 20-seater bought in 1928

United Counties route 345, via Bugbrooke to Northampton
passing through Gayton at 7.55 am, Spring 1982

Arthur Roberts' bus

The first bus to run regularly through Gayton belonged to Mr Kirton of Eastcote in 1923. Five years later Arthur Roberts started a service in 1928 which ran from the village via Blisworth, Milton Malsor to Northampton, and like today's minbus, his bus provided a community service. When the Mothers' Union was invited to an event in Greens Norton on 3 July 1928 they arranged to be taken in the brand new bus. Roberts' second bus, which he had bought only 12 months earlier, went up in flames on 13 June 1933. The garage at his home, Sunnymead, caught fire and only through his neighbours prompt action was the bungalow saved. With the loss of his business he went to work for United Counties. But his life still had dramatic moments. On the way to work he saw two boys fall into the river Nene. He dived in, pulled them out and left quickly as he was late for work and now had to go home to change his clothes. As he told no-one of the incident he lost part of that day's money and it was not until much later that people knew of his brave rescue.

Mervyn Cockerill at his home on Eastcote Road in the early 1950s

Rose Inns at the Banbury Lane Crossing c1900

The bicycle

The bicycle enabled people to travel further, more easily, without the drawback of feeding and watering it like a horse! Bicycling became a popular past-time and in 1914 Walter Frost profited from the new craze by advertising the Crown and Squirrel as having good accommodation for cyclists and parties.

The state of the roads

In the 1920s the roads were dirty and rutted as they were mainly used by horses, carts and animals. Motor vehicles were few and far between although some breweries did use steam driven lorries. When Harold Morgan rode his bicycle on the footpath, his defence that the road was muddy was not accepted by Towcester Petty Sessions. The action was regarded as dangerous and he was fined six shillings by the court.

Evelyn Cockerill with a friend at Brittains Cottages c1936

The canal came to Gayton

By boat from Birmingham to London through Gayton

Transportation and communication improved with the building of the canals. When the Grand Junction canal was built to connect the Oxford canal at Braunston to London, it passed through Gayton. Work was started in 1793 and the canal had progressed through Gayton to Blisworth by 1796. The problems encountered in tunnelling through the Blisworth Hill to Stoke Bruerne held up the work. The tunnel, and therefore the entire canal, was delayed until Monday 25 March 1805, when finally Birmingham was linked with London. However, canal traffic passing through Gayton had started to grow from 1796. At the height of canal transport 70 or 80 boats a day were travelling through the parish.

An exciting and bustling place

The Anchor Inn opened to catch the new passing trade. Each boat travelling the canal was operated by two men and a horse. They all required feeding. By 1911 the Anchor had 18 stables and a blacksmith's shop which shod horses and repaired boats. In addition ropes, candles and other general goods were needed. Some of the traffic was local business making use of the new lines of communication. Local breweries, for example, began delivering beer by boat and the brickworks and ironworks found the canal suitable for their needs. It must have been an exciting development for villagers giving them more job opportunities, and the canal boats often picked up passing passengers.

A tragic accident

At the same time, however, there were disadvantages. The canal gave easy access to the village and no doubt strange and disreputable individuals came to Gayton horrifying the inhabitants and preying on them. Accidents happened as well, for example, on 13 January 1936 there was a fatality on the canal when Mrs Owen, employed on a motor barge travelling from London to Birmingham, was accidentally drowned at Banbury Lane.

Life near the canal

Heavy goods came by canal

It was the easy transportation of heavy goods that really made the difference to ordinary peoples' lives. Crockery from Staffordshire became available. Roadstone from Leicestershire arrived and local roads were improved. Blue slate from Wales (as well as from Collyweston) began to replace the thatched roofing. Dr Butler had a slate roof put on the brand new village school in 1846.

Coal transformed village life

Coal from the mines of Derbyshire, Yorkshire and Nottinghamshire provided cheap fuel for the farm labourer. Thomas Cockerill was the first coal merchant to deliver from Banbury Lane Wharf until his premature death in 1812. Then, John Chamberlain combined running the Anchor Inn with being a coal merchant, running a wharf and a 46 acre farm until

Wright's Lane bridge c1910

Geofrey Golding, Winnie Faulkner, Leslie, Ron and Cyril Hillyer playing in the boat turn-around in the 1920s

William George Newcomb working on the canal c1940

Steam waggon collecting granite chippings brought by canal boat

1852. His son-in-law, Richard Gardener, who had been working as a coal porter for many years, took over the business. However, he found he preferred running the pub and quickly moved on to the Crown and Squirrel. James Ayres Wootton, who had been operating the Outdoor Beerhouse at 1 High Street, by 1866 had moved to the Banbury Lane enterprises. Between 1871 and 1874 George Savage of Stoke Bruerne bought the Anchor Inn and installed William Taylor as manager. Eventually he split the business retaining the Anchor Inn and wharf, whilst selling the coal interests to George Kingston, a member of the family who ran the village carriers business. Finally at the beginning of the twentieth century the coal merchant's was taken over by John Manning Payne who lived in the centre of the village in Payne's Yard. By 1926 coal had become necessary to people's well being. This was illustrated by Revd Stokes' comments in the parish magazine that 'scarcity of coal was proving a trial in the village' and that he hoped the situation would change before the cold weather set in.

Enter the railway

By train from Birmingham to London through Gayton

Hot on the heels of the canal came the railway. First a large army of navvies camped in huts along Robert Stephenson's proposed route, parallel to the canal. These men built the railways with only picks, shovels, horses and carts to move the tons of earth. They were paid well for their work and were known for drinking their wages away. It would not have been too far for them to walk to the beerhouses in Gayton, probably bringing fighting and brawling to the streets during their temporary stay in the neighbourhood.

Six trains a day

By 1838, 42 years after the arrival of the canal, the London and Birmingham Railway opened. Four trains daily were 'express' trains, travelling the 112.5 miles in 5 hours 37 minutes at an average speed of 19 miles per hour. Previously the journey would have taken two days and included an overnight stop. The train arrived at Blisworth 3 hours and 11 minutes into the journey. The locomotives were regarded with trepidation by the population who thought their livestock would be terrified by the iron monsters, worried that the woods would be set on fire by sparks from the boilers, and horrified at the speed of the locomotives.

Passengers were most uncomfortable

The rails were laid on stone blocks which gave a rough ride with frequent jolts and bumps. But there was a respite for ten minutes at Wolverton where the passengers were able to make use of the newly built refreshment rooms which were open day and night. The London and Birmingham Railway became the London and North Western Railway and this service still runs today as part of the Inter-City Network. Mr John Adams-Evans, (born in Gayton and whose father was killed locally on the LNWR) was the guard on the train that made the fastest time. This was the London to Aberdeen express on 13 August 1895 which covered the 540 miles in 518 minutes. He retired in 1914 after working for the company for 40 years and in recognition the directors doubled his pension.

Sacked and homeless

In the 1880s when the Billinghams lived at the Anchor Inn they were expected to welcome travellers who had been set down from the train at the Banbury Crossing. Late one night some important people were dropped off at the Crossing. They knocked at the door of the Anchor but were unable to rouse anybody. The exhausted Billingham family were all deeply asleep. The next day the Billinghams were evicted. It seems unthinkable today that not only were trains allowed to stop at crossings, but people were summarily made homeless.

The Banbury Lane in its hey-day. The farm buildings and outhouses are visible to the left of the main house which used to be the Anchor Inn and in 2000 is a private house. Canal workers lived in the cottages on the right. The railway cottages can just be seen to the left of the signal box. The farm cottages, on the far right, have been demolished.

Lightening strikes community

The settlement at Banbury Lane had grown up due to the ancient drovers' road being crossed by the canal and then the railway. It became a bustling commercial centre serving the Gayton wharf, a farm, a brickworks and a coal merchants. While the transport systems flourished, they altered the focal point of the village. However tragedy struck the community on Thursday 22 August 1895 when Gayton was hit by a monstrous thunderstorm. All around the village people woke up in the early morning and looked out, but it was the Anchor Inn at the Banbury Crossing that was destined to suffer.

A blue ball of fire

Although it was half past four in the morning, Mr George Inns, aged 47, was looking out of the window of the railway cottages at the fateful moment. He was signalman on the LNWR railway and father of five children who were crying and frightened by the force of the gale. His account at the inquest, held at the Anchor Inn itself, must have brought the whole scene to life. George Inns told of a flash of lightening which turned into a ball of blue fire. It travelled, slowly, horizontally, before striking something and exploding. George Webb lived at the Anchor and worked as a shepherd. His wife, Eliza Ann, and a niece who lived with them ran the pub. Mrs Webb was terrified of lightening and had been so disturbed by the storm that she and her husband had both got up. He had blacked out and when he came round found his wife unconscious on the floor. As she showed no signs of life he

George Inns at the old signal box, Banbury Crossing, where he worked and also grew cyclamens!

A bridge over the disused Northampton and Banbury Junction railway in 1991

called for assistance after laying her on the bed. Mr Lawton the surgeon from Bugbrooke explained that an upstairs window frame had shattered and the lightening had travelled across the room into a bedroom where it had struck Mrs Webb. Her hair had been singed just behind her right ear causing her death to follow from shock.

Banbury Lane crossing

Once a strategic site, the Banbury Lane community became isolated with the demise of the canal and the advent of the through train. A continental style gate was installed on 30 June 1964. In 1999 Railtrack tried to close the crossing to cars and pedestrians due to the increased number and speed of trains. However, in the light of local public dismay they have agreed to build a road bridge.

The Northampton and Banbury Junction railway

A second railway company built another line that passed to the east of the parish of Gayton. On Saturday 28 April 1866 the section opened from Blisworth to Towcester through Gayton. This line was extended through Banbury and was taken over by the Stratford-on-Avon and Midland Junction Railway company who reduced the journey time from Towcester to Banbury by 15 minutes. Passenger services operated for 86 years finishing on Saturday 5 April 1952 but the link was still used for transporting goods until May 1958. The rails were lifted between 1962 and 1964 and the rolling stock was sold off. Old railway carriages can still be seen in unexpected places around the village serving in a new life as a garden shed or storehouse. The disused railway itself offers an ideal habitat for wild animals and is part of a nature reserve created by John Mawby.

Railway wagons were sold off when the Northampton and Banbury Junction railway was closed. This one was moved to Evergreen Farm.

Nothing changes! The gates on the LNWR line always seem to be closed.

The thrill of the motorbike

Margaret Ratledge at the Weir

Bert Cockerill on his home-made grass track motorcycle. The tyres were stuffed with grass because inner tubes were unavailable in the mid 1930s.

Motorbikes outside the Queen Victoria were a regular sight when Brian Cross was the landlord

Harry Cockerill with Molly Moore, pillion, and her friend

The Local

Were there many pubs?

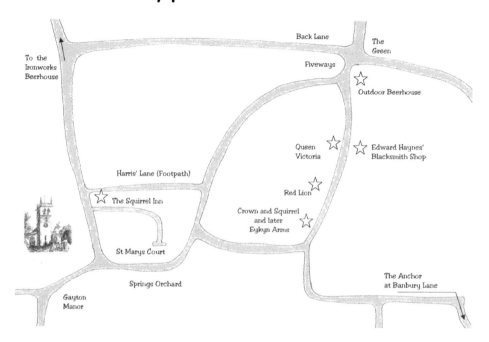

Eight pubs

George Reeve ran the earliest documented alehouse in Gayton in 1673. Another appeared briefly in the mid-eighteenth century run by Thomas Dunckley, and the Anchor Inn opened in response to the canal being built. It was not until the nineteenth century that Gayton was spoiled for choice. In 1830, to revive its failing popularity and to encourage the population to drink beer rather than spirits, the government passed the Beer Act. This made acquiring a licence to open a beerhouse easier. The Queen Victoria and Red Lion both grew from shops branching out as a direct response to the Act. Two much smaller enterprises, the 'Outdoor Beerhouse' and Edward Haynes blacksmith's shop, took advantage of the easing of restrictions to supplement the family income.

The Squirrel Inn

The Squirrel became the Squirrel and Crown, then the Crown and Squirrel until today, in a different location and called the Eykyn Arms, it continues as a popular village pub. In 1701 Richard Rogers, left the Squirrel Inn to his daughter-in-law Margaret Houghton. She married Thomas Wilson in Gayton Church soon afterwards. Margaret survived her husband by 31 years and supervised the running of the Squirrel through two generations of her family.

Named to flatter the Lord of the Manor

The name of the inn probably originated from the squirrel on the Samwell coat of arms and crest. The Wilson family, who owned the pub, needed the support of the Samwells, (lords of the manor 1607-1751) to run a successful business.

Cockfighting

The Samwell family enjoyed cockfighting and competed against other county families. By offering this entertainment in 1741 the Squirrel attracted the custom of the gentry. Although prohibited by law, cockfighting was so widely popular that it was not suppressed until 1849.

What did the Squirrel look like?

In 1762 the description was brief, 'barns, stables, garden, and orchard', but it was expanded in 1803 to:

> The Premises consist of spacious Hall, two excellent Parlours, Kitchen, and Wash-house, with Oven in the same, on the Ground Floor; five Chambers on the first Floor, with Attics over Ditto; good Brew-house and Pump of excellent Water, large Barn, Stabling, paved Yard and Pump of good Water, two Gardens and large Orchard well planned with choice Fruit Trees. - Also a COTTAGE, containing two Rooms on the Ground Floor, with an Oven, and two Chambers, a Garden, and Wood-Shed.

By 1877 the Squirrel had moved to new premises in the High Street. The yard now had a coach house, stables and blacksmith's shop and indoors downstairs, following modernisation, there was a bar, tap room and two front parlours, and upstairs were two clubrooms and four bed rooms.

Extreme poverty

When villagers no longer buy beer, it is a sign of hard times. John Smith, a man from outside the village, took over the licence of the Squirrel in 1793 with Thomas West a Gayton farmer backing him. By 1803 Smith was bankrupt. Rural poverty was evident and in 1819 two of the village men were prosecuted for abandoning their wives and families. William Kingston was discharged but Samuel Dunckley was sent to Northampton Gaol for one week's hard labour.

Benjamin George

A local family, the Cockerills took over the Squirrel's licence. Ann Cockerill married James Ide, a carpenter, in 1817 and became the landlady. Her husband died very young and she re-married and continued running the pub with her new husband Benjamin George who was a butcher and farmer from Northampton. The Rector, Dr Butler, may have found Benjamin George 'most troublesome' but the Georges ran the business successfully for the next two decades.

Moving house

During the nineteenth century a change of site provided the Crown and Squirrel with a central location. Being closer to the increasingly affluent farmers and tradesmen, on whose trade it now became dependent, was critical to its survival through to this day.

Landlords of the Eykyn Arms
Martha and Walter Frost ran the Eykyn Arms 1914-24. Martha ran the business whilst Walter could turn his hand to anything. He was carpenter, undertaker, painter and house decorator.

Walter Frost, landlord

Martha Frost outside the Eykyn Arms

The Back Bar at the Eykyn Arms

Left to right: Viv Bailey, Jackie Huckerby with landlord Ron Hiscocke

The Back Bar at the Eykyn Arms in 1978

Left to right: Martin and Sonia Church, Thelma Mansfield and Eric Cockerill

The circus

Most pubs provided relatively cheap accommodation. One of the Frosts' lodgers, who worked at Fossett's Circus, (the circus that wintered its animals on the farm next to the road into Tiffield) provided an added attraction. For a wager one day, he climbed onto the roof of the pub and stood on his head on one of the chimneys. Fossett's hit the news in November 1939 when the elephant that had starred in *Elephant Boy* suddenly died. It was being used for wartime propaganda from its winter home in Tiffield.

Queen Victoria

William Facer's shop

William Facer, who was born in Kislingbury, moved to a house in the centre of the village, and established a grocer's shop. He applied for a licence on 31 December 1817 to use his premises as a meeting house for religious worship for dissenting Protestants. The shop expanded into selling beer and a bakery was added to the grocery business. Eventually William Facer opened a beerhouse which may fleetingly have been known as the Queen Adelaide but it settled on the name of Queen Victoria. A yard of eight houses known as Facer's Yard was built alongside.

The Queen Victoria and shop c1914

Typhus fever

William and Lucy's 11 year old daughter, Susan was their youngest child and she died on 30 May 1851. She probably contracted typhus fever which was rampant in the village at the time. William Facer died and was buried in Gayton churchyard on 6 March 1862, aged 81.

The Queen Victoria

This view of the Queen Victoria has a horse and cart alongside
the remaining cottage of a row of old cottages

Henry and Edith Wakelin ran the Queen Victoria
and shop in 1931

Although there is some uncertainty, this may be a very old
photograph of the Queen Victoria

Pub, bakehouse, shop and Chapel

The business was put up for sale following William's death. It was a large concern having two cellars, a tap room, kitchen, front shop, two parlours, and five bedrooms together with a bakehouse, meal chambers, a good yard, two stables, a brewhouse and other outbuildings including the large garden. Also for sale was Facer's Yard, eight cottages that were being rented by Messrs Facer, Chamberlain, Dunckley and Webb, and 'others'. A building was also included, 'that had hitherto been used as a Chapel'.

Phipps Brewery

Phipps Brewery bought the pub but Lucy continued running the business which passed on down the generations. Thomas, her eldest son, returned to Gayton with his wife Elizabeth, (née Muscott), when Lucy could manage no longer. By 1891 Thomas had died and his widow Elizabeth, now aged 74, was helped by her married daughter Emma Brocklis and granddaughter Eliza Facer.

Pub games

The villagers entertained themselves with an assortment of games. Skittles, dominoes, peg board, cards and a new twentieth-century game, darts, were all played in the parlour. Most popular were the betting games such as tippit. One team bet on their skill to pass a button from fist to fist between them, aiming to mislead the opposing team as to its whereabouts. The other team bet on their skill to follow the button's progress. Every round would be celebrated with the drinking of beer at each other's expense.

Brian Cross, landlord (1966-77)

Brian Cross ran a busy popular pub. He made many changes but perhaps the closing of the shop was the one most regretted by villagers. When the lounge was extended, a time capsule of beer mats, money, photos, beer bottles and cans was placed into a girder and has remained undisturbed throughout the 1999 alterations.

Thomas Dunckley's beerhouse

The site of Thomas Dunckley's beerhouse has not been located but it operated from approximately 1740-60. It increased the number of drinking houses in Gayton at a time when the national consumption of liquor was growing.

The Anchor Inn

Edward Phipps

When Edward Phipps opened the Anchor Inn trade was good and he became affluent. His estate was valued at £1000 when he died in 1826. Phipps and his wife, Mary, ran the Inn for over 30 years. As his brother was Pickering Phipps, the Towcester and Northampton brewer, and the business was not taken over by the Phipps Company but by the

Brian Cross, landlord of the Queen Victoria

neighbouring coal merchant, John Chamberlain in 1849, it is likely that its custom was already declining. Even so, the coal dealer's business, with its contingent of carriers' carts, undoubtedly bolstered trade.

Anchor House which used to be the Anchor Inn

Overnight lodgings
The Anchor catered mainly for the travelling workmen requiring basic accommodation with no frills. It is not difficult to see that these customers did not expect the same style as those encountered at the Squirrel, indeed the priority requirement seems to have been outdoors rather than inside. On 13 May 1911 the Anchor Inn was described as having 'a bar, tap-room, sitting room, scullery, five good bedrooms, two attics, beer cellars, a store-room with a loft over, two large spacious yards and outbuildings, comprising stable accommodation for 18 horses, a blacksmith's shop, pigstys, a chaff-house, cart hovel, large store or warehouse with loft over and wharf'.

Eighteen stables
The stabling facilities would have been for canal boat horses. As one horse would pull a boat 20 miles, there was a constant turnover of horses. This transport system declined and soon after the beginning of the twentieth century the Anchor Inn stopped trading and became a private home.

Beer by canal
A passageway went from Gayton Wharf under the road straight into the Anchor's cellars enabling the barrels of beer to be delivered by canal.

Haynes the blacksmith

Edward Haynes owned a blacksmith shop in 1849, in High Street. His son, William, had taken over by 1869 and probably in an effort to make ends meet entered the beer retailing market. It seems likely that he was a blacksmith first and foremost and it was not until 1885 that he advertised his beer retailing business.

The Ironworks' beerhouse

The White House was school teacher, George Dixon's home. His son, Frank, opened a lunch-time beerhouse there, between 1875 and 1900, at the height of the ironstone operations. A beerhouse needed to be close to its community and this was very close to the workings. Frank Dixon served beer solely for the convenience of the ironstone workers. Joseph Montague Major Lucas lived at the White House c1930 until his death in 1948 aged 86. He had been choirmaster and churchwarden for 32 years.

The White House was used as a beerhouse for
the ironworkers at lunchtime

1 High Street

In 1858 James Ayres Wootton was the publican who started the beer retailing tradition at 1 High Street. His two sons both worked in trades allied to beer selling. One was a baker and the other a blacksmith. The baker uses yeast, just as the brewer does and it was traditional to drink beer whilst waiting for the blacksmith to shoe the horse. James moved on to the Anchor Inn at the same time as Frederick Wootton was running the Crown and Squirrel. By 1881 James had left Gayton and Frederick Wootton had turned his hand to being the village shoemaker.

John Moore the Carrier
Yew Tree House, or 1 High Street, was known locally as the Jug and Bottle and had a prime site at the centre of the village at Fiveways. This made buying a jug of beer to drink with a meal at home a simple task. John Moore moved in and combined the beerhouse with his business which in 1869 was at the 'top end' of the Gayton carrier business. More often than not he would have been transporting people as well as goods every Wednesday to the Black Boy, Northampton. What could be more natural than on arriving home after a day at Northampton market than to purchase some beer with which to relax in the evening?

1, High Street c1890 was licensed to sell beer and also had a blacksmith's shop attached

1, High Street in 1994 as a private residence. The beerhouse had ceased trading in 1954.

Even today the carrier's cart (sorry, the Gayton and Tiffield minibus!) starts its journey from outside 1 High Street. Volunteer drivers and organisers have provided Gayton and Tiffield with a bus service to Northampton, Towcester and Milton Keynes since 23 May 1984.

The Red Lion

Thomas and Mary Payne's shop
A cottage called 'an ancient messuage' in 1826 had been occupied by George Hook, followed by Samuel Maddock and then Widow Kingston (John Kingston's wife). Behind this old dwelling, Thomas Dunckley built two cottages on land sold to him by William Facer. In 1826 Thomas Farrin and Richard Benjamin were living there. The two cottages were knocked into one and Thomas and Mary Payne moved in and opened their shop in about 1830. Thomas and Mary Payne united two established Gayton families, the Paynes and the Dunckleys. When they opened a beerhouse, the Red Lion, their family connections ensured them of a certain section of the beer drinking market. Whilst the house had no cellars it did have a private well, hence the modern name, Well House.

Generations of landlords
When Thomas Payne senior died in 1860, his son Thomas and wife Elizabeth returned to Gayton to continue running the business. In 1878 it was described as 'a freehold beerhouse and premises known as the Red Lion situate at Gayton and freehold cottage adjoining'. Thomas died in 1883 and Elizabeth in 1886, and their son Thomas Payne with his wife Lucy, followed in their footsteps until Thomas' death in 1923. The Paynes ran the Red Lion successfully through three generations, spanning 70 years, possibly longer.

The Red Lion pub, which in 2000 is a private residence called Well House

Hops

The alehouses brewing their own beer required hops. However, hops were susceptible to pest and fungus attack, making them an uncertain and difficult crop. The best hops came from Kent and the Woolpack Inn in Bridge Street in Northampton traded in these, making them readily available locally. However, whilst the Gudgeon family were the maltsters, living in Gayton House was John Darker who had worked in London as a hop merchant.

Crime in Gayton

There has always been been a strong connection between crime and drink in the minds of those in authority. One story links crime in Gayton with drink. On 5 November 1898, Henry Bennett, aged 49 and a shoe laster from Coventry with seven previous convictions for drunkeness, had obtained by false pretences, beer and tobacco from Gayton and Blisworth. He must have been an exceptional con-man as he acquired at least seven pints of beer, at 2d a pint, on credit from Alice Chester, wife of Frank Chester, at the Crown and Squirrel, and a similar amount of beer plus tobacco from Elizabeth Facer at the Queen Victoria. His method sheds light on life in a small village. He told Alice that he had been working for William George who had sent him for some beer and George would call in and pay her later.

The Maltster

Barley for brewing

The maltster must have been an important man in the lives of the various beerhouses whilst they were brewing their own beer. John Allen, a weaver, lived in the millhouse and, in August 1608, owned the adjoining malt mill with its millstones, as well as a windmill south of the village and the willow and osier beds necessary to his trade. In 1716 Revd William Gibbs owned a malt mill, barley and other paraphernalia. Cornelius Gudgeon was the village maltster until his death in 1764 when John Gudgeon combined it with being a shoemaker until 1789. John Cockerill with his son Thomas took over the maltster role and when John Cockerill died, in 1802, William Watson took over.

Landlord of the Crown and Squirrel

Later John West who married Elizabeth Watson became maltster and landlord of the Crown and Squirrel as well. The Wests, in 1841, rented the Dower House, a substantial house, from Elizabeth Coleman. A gravestone in the churchyard reveals their heartbreakingly sad family life and also the high rate of infant mortality. 'Walter West, son of John and Elizabeth West, died at 10 years old in 1853'. At the bottom is the simple comment, 'and of eight children of the above parents who died in their infancy'.

Church connections

Thomas and Elizabeth Coleman lived next door to the old dairy across the road from Evergreen Farm. They owned land and the Dower House which was rented as early as 1820 to Edward Schrivener. It is possible that Dr Butler purchased it as accommodation for the curate when he was made Dean in 1842 as his family continued to live at the Rectory in Gayton. Certainly the Dower House has a cross and religious text very similar to the schoolhouse which Butler had built in 1846.

From Deanery to Dower House

When Revd Whitehurst lived there it was called Gayton cottage. By 1891 it was called the Deanery and owned by Rowland M Estcote a barrister. Arthur Eykyn bought it a few years later renting it to a parade of the well-to-do, Lord William Beresford, the Duchess of Newcastle, the Padmores and then the Crocketts. Sometime after 1923 Mrs Eykyn moved in and the house became known as the Dower House.

Reputedly owned at one time by Dr Butler, the house was renamed the Dower House
when Mrs Eykyn moved in

Homes with Character

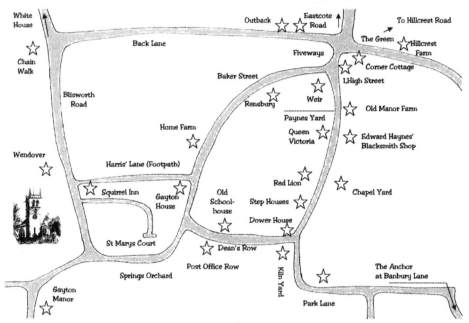

Map of the centre of Gayton and location of cottages

A hundred years ago the village was made up of small yards and rows of cottages branching off the High Street. From Fiveways down to the old schoolhouse, was Payne's Yard, Facer's Yard, Green's Yard, Chapel Yard, Kiln Yard, and Middleton's Yard to name but a few! Over the years they changed their names. Payne's Yard had been Griffith's Yard and before that Stone Leys Yard. There was Post Office Row, which before the arrival of the Post Office was called Doctor's Row, and others which have long since disappeared such as Orange Row and Rabbit Row. Each of these was a little community.

Kiln Yard

Between the wars, Kiln Yard was a row of six old terraced cottages which backed onto Park Lane. It was once Hawley-owned but sold to the Eykyn family. A few of the cottages had slate roofs whilst those nearer Deans Row were thatched. The row faced onto a cobbled yard with drains down the middle. On the far side of the yard was a row of outhouses, one for each house, and on the end of the row was another cottage. Its corrugated iron roof can just be seen in the photograph on page 36. In the small side garden, as well as the privy, was holly, and a plum tree that still survives today. The earth closets for the other houses were through an overgrown, permanently open, rusty iron gate and down a stone walled footpath which was close to the fields and on rough ground near a pond. Quite a way to walk, in the dark, clutching only a candle to light your way!

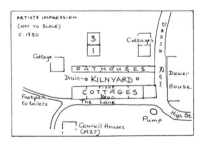

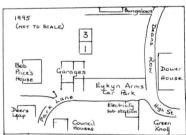

Sketches of Kiln Yard in 1930 and 1995

Mrs Edith Wakelin in the garden of the council houses in Park Lane. The back of the end houses in Kiln Yard, furthest from Deans Row, can be seen behind her c1930.

Cooking over the fire

Each cottage had an open fireplace to cook on. There was a hob on either side on which to stand pots and a container for heating water. This had a tap to allow hot water to be run off - when it worked! An ash preventer stopped the hot ashes from falling out of the fire on to the cook. Oil lamps lit the houses and although gas came into the village in the mid-1930s, Kiln Yard was never to benefit from it.

Large families

Two cottages at the Dower House end of Kiln Yard had been occupied by the Tomalin family, who were followed by the Cokaynes, and Mr Mcknight, an old gentleman with a wooden leg who had retired from the Chinese police force. The Eykyns had these two houses knocked into one to accommodate nurses, such as Nurse Ladkin, who looked after the well-to-do ladies of the village. There were children everywhere. Next door to the large Tomalin family lived Mr and Mrs Paul with their six children, Mr and Mrs Jacobs with their two boys, and Mr and Mrs Moore with their four children.

Colin Wakelin is learning to fetch water for his grandmother,
Martha Rook, from the pump in Post Office Row c1930

Mr Bolton fought in Crimea

At the far end of the row lived Mr Bolton who, in 1856, had been a major in the Northamptonshire Regiment and fought in the Crimean War. Mr Bolton was unlikely to have forgotten the cheering crowds when, bearded, moustached and bronzed the Militia arrived home at Northampton station. He died, aged 92, and was buried with full military honours, at the instigation of the churchwarden, Mr Major-Lucas. A detachment of the Regiment acted as bearers and sounded the last post. A gun salute was fired over the grave in the churchyard. Revd Hugh King, who had been an officer in the Regiment himself, took the service in the absence of his father who was Gayton's Rector.

My hat!
Mr Kendrick, who lived at the far end of the row of outhouses would finish chatting to the neighbours with the words, 'Well, I must go and change now'. He would disappear into his cottage and emerge a little later having changed his cap! Later Mr and Mrs Newcomb moved into that cottage, with their three children, Walter, Ray and Margaret.

R101 over Gayton
Walter Newcomb remembers the day in 1930 when the people of Kiln Yard were joined by most of the village to watch, what was to be, the ill-fated R101 airship. It flew down the valley, from the north, on its way back towards its hangar at Cardington. Walter was only a small child at the time and recalls standing on the stone wall to watch, whilst Hilda Billing, who was at school, remembers the whole school running outside to look at this novelty flying over the fields. Later in 1930, the R101 crashed and put paid to Britain's airship building programme. Just think, the whole village turned out to see a plane!

Wash day blues
Mrs Jacobs was a likeable woman. She had a red and purple fuschia bush by her front door and kept chickens on the land further down the lane. To help support the family she took in washing. The doctor from Blisworth was one of her customers. Day after day she was to be seen in her outhouse in the yard doing piles and piles of washing. How she managed to get it all dry in the winter was a mystery. Mrs Jacobs made good use of the Kiln Yard pump. All the water used in the cottages had to be carried in by the bucketful from an iron pump opposite the Dower House, on the corner of Park Lane and High Street, where the electricity sub-station is today.

A crystal radio
The Jacobs family was the first in the row to have a crystal radio. Every evening Mr Fisher, who had moved into Mr Bolton's house, would sidle up to the Jacobs' window to set his pocket watch by the six o'clock pips which could be heard in Kiln Yard.

No central heating!
Imagine living in a house with no electricity or gas, only oil lamps or candle light. Imagine no running water, only a big old iron pump and no sink, only a few drains in the yard. Imagine no cooker, only an open wood fire or range and no indoor plumbing, only some outside toilets at the bottom of the lane. Hilda Billing still occasionally dreams that she is standing in the lane peeping through the window which was fringed with lace curtains and looking inside at the stone floor and the wooden staircase, which was riddled with woodworm.

Park Lane

The four 'non-parlour' type council houses in Park Lane were built in 1921 under the assisted housing scheme of 1919, by Towcester Rural District Council (TRDC). By 1933 the houses were providing good quality homes at a rent of 5s 6d per week. However, rural workers were poorly paid and this was more than they could easily afford.

Four council houses in Park Lane were built in 1921

Neighbours in the council houses,
Park Lane c1930
Left to right: Thelma Mansfield, Edie Paul, Fred
Mansfield with baby Bernard in the wheelbarrow and
Pam Mansfield

Step Houses

Next to the Eykyn Arms was Vic Rook's house and a row of condemned cottages that were sold by the Eykyn family on Wednesday 18 September 1957, as part of the Dower House Estate. Vic Rook bought his house, and later the cottages, which he demolished to provide himself with a garden.

Step Houses with Ivy Cottage set back and the
Eykyn Arms further along High Street

The 1977 Jubilee celebrations near Ivy Cottage,
24 years after Step Houses were demolished

'Junk on' Jimmy

Step Houses, next to the Eykyn Arms on High Street, were occupied c1912 by Jimmy Clarke, Mrs Botterill and Jimmy Billingham. The latter was a very small man who was a real character. He was a roundabout attendant, probably with Fossett's Circus. Instead of calling out 'Jump on' he shouted 'Junk on' and became known locally as Jimmy 'Junk on'. As a prank one day, some children in the village tied the doors of the Step Houses to one another. When his door wouldn't open Jimmy called out to the children, 'Wait till I got my second Sunday-best shoes on and I'll arter yer and run yer to hell'.

In the coffin

Mr Shakeshaft, the landlord of the Eykyn Arms before Walter Frost, was also an undertaker. It was a common sight to see him polishing the coffins on the taproom table. On one occasion he hid Jimmy 'Junk on' inside a coffin giving his regulars the shock of their lives when the coffin lid began to open!

No back way

Electricity had arrived in the village in 1929. Although the cottages were extremely old when Mrs Griffin, Miss Wakelin and Cyril Hillyer were living there, they had been connected to the electricity supply. But water still had to be fetched from the pump at the corner of High Street and Park Lane. As the cottages had no back way, all night soil and refuse had to be carried through the parlour which resulted in them being condemned.

Chapel Yard in the early 1930s

Chapel Yard was a group of two red-brick houses, a chapel and six stone cottages on the land next to Evergreen Stables, and on the site of today's Post Office and its neighbours. The overwhelming recollection of the inhabitants was of a happy life.

Wash day

Monday was wash day. Mary and Harry George, like other children, were sent to the pump to fetch buckets of water before school. Their mother, Ethel, had a large pot over the fire in which she boiled the sheets. When they were deemed clean, they were rinsed and carried down the garden to be hung on the line to dry. Washing was hard physical work which took all day. Boiling the clothes over a fire in a tiny cottage took time. When the children returned from school, the scullery was full of dirty dishes which had accumulated during the day and they were expected to wash them up. Dinner on wash day was invariably bubble and squeak followed by rice pudding.

Charlie Rook

Charlie Rook was notorious for propping the pump handle up with a stone to keep the water flowing. Eventually water poured over the top of his bucket but, eager though the children were to finish their chores, none of them would dare to remove the stone and bucket, but had to wait until Charlie returned.

Chapel Yard on High Street

Charlie Rook in his garden

Gardens

Behind the chapel, each cottage had a plot of garden, although some plots were bigger than others. The Georges' was at the bottom where Jack kept a pig and some hens, and Ethel hung her washing. Hilda Rook, Charlie's wife, loved growing flowers and her garden was her pride and joy. Hilda had spent all one morning setting carnation cuttings when a child, Barbara Moore, came along and pulled them all up. Her mother, Gladys, was distraught when she found out about her daughter's vandalism and with 'Georgie' (Ethel) set to work replanting them before Hilda discovered the mayhem.

Chapel Yard families formed a tiny, tight community

People moved in and out of Chapel Yard frequently but in living memory there has been Charlie and Hilda Rook, Vic and Bessie Rook, Tom and Gladys Moore, Barbara and Binnie, Mr and Mrs Arnold Webb and Ron, Ethel and Jack George with Mary and Harry, and two families of Cowleys. When Mr and Mrs Pankcost, Eunice, Reg and Gwen moved out they were replaced by Frank and Hilda Wakelin and Colin. They took over the running of the Eykyn Arms, and Mr and Mrs Smith, Lou and Freda moved in. In the summer, when the evenings were light, after the children had gone to bed, the adults would sit out in the Yard, eating bread, cheese and pickled onions and gossiping together until late into the night.

Door to door salesmen

Living so far away from the town did not stop door to door salesmen calling. One man walked all the way from Northampton with a wicker basket on wheels selling second-hand clothes. Another door to door caller earned his pennies by standing on his head in a bucket and singing Nellie Dean!

A Cockerill Christmas

Harry George remembered Christmas as a family time. Christmas lunch was eaten at home in Chapel Yard. At 3pm his family gathered at Grey House in Baker Street, the home of William and Sarah Cockerill, his grandparents. They had a tea of home cured ham, pork pies, trifle and Christmas cake before his uncle, who was a good pub pianist, provided the accompaniment to a sing-song and a knees-up which made the walls shake.

High Street and Payne's Yard

The 'Rubbish House'

On 29 January 1916 a party was held in the Post Office to celebrate the Golden Wedding Anniversary of Mr John Tomalin, 74, and Emma, his wife. They still lived in the cottage in High Street, opposite the Queen Victoria, where Mrs Tomalin (née Floyd) was born 69 years earlier. By the 1930s this house had been unoccupied for some time and had become known as 'the rubbish house'. As part of the war effort newspaper was stored there. Barbara Moore and Ivy White pushed an old pram, door to door, on Friday afternoons collecting the newspapers. Eventually they were taken to Rolls' stables (which used to be next to the footpath called Harris' Lane) to be sorted by Edie Cockerill and Gladys Moore.

The Tomalin's cottage, later known as the 'Rubbish House'

Payne's Yard

Only part of the outside walls remain of two brick-fronted cottages on the right-hand corner of Payne's Yard with High Street. These were demolished during the Second World War after being used as an exercise area for fire and rescue. Smoke bombs were thrown into the empty houses and dummies 'rescued' from the ensuing 'disaster'. It was a harsh reminder of what many evacuees had suffered and frightened the village children. Next door a row of six terraced cottages led down to Primrose Cottage, once called Stone Leys. The last cottage was set forward from the rest of the row, (pictured right), and was owned by Daisy and Bert Cockerill (Denis Cockerill's parents) in the 1930s. All that remains is the line of slabs that once served as the front path to the cottages. On the left of the yard, next door to the Queen Victoria, were two brick built cottages, once the homes of Olive Billing and Tom Powell. These have been knocked into one house, Sunnyside, and pebble dashed.

Next door to the Weir

There were two cottages owned by Elizabeth Ratledge, and adjoining to the Weir, which was named after an ancient pond in High Street. The cottage closest to the Weir was occupied by Mr and Mrs Arthur Barker. The other was called Rose Cottage and occupied by Mr and Mrs Jack Sturgess in the 1930s before they moved further down the High Street. These cottages were not pulled down until the 1960s.

Weir Cottages being demolished c1964

The Payne family outside their house in Payne's Yard

On the corner of Payne's Yard and High Street was a prefabricated bungalow erected in the mid-1920s and pulled down in 1964. At one end a brick outhouse served as a scullery and at the other end another housed a bucket toilet, which was emptied on to the garden.

Snow clearing in High Street c1900

Snow clearing in 1947

Cockerill Family in Baker Street c1936

Left to right:

Back row	Bert Pearson, unknown, William (Tom) Cockerill jnr, Mary Nightingale, Elsie Cockerill, Unity Pearson, Mary Pearson
Next row	Ellen (Nell) Cockerill, Brenda Cockerill, Ethel (Lil) Cockerill, Annie (Nance) Jacobs
Middle row	William Thomas Cockerill and Sarah Cockerill
Front row	Ted Cockerill behind son Eric, Eddie Spencer, William (Bill) Jacobs, Raymond Cockerill, Dot Cockerill with baby Barry

Clearance Order

On 28 August 1934 a clearance order was served on the following:

- two houses in High Street owned by Elizabeth Ratledge

- one house in Payne's Yard owned by Ivy Morgan and occupied by Walter George

- four houses owned by Daisy Cockerill and occupied by Thomas Green, Owen Castle, James Hillyer and Albert Cockerill

- two houses in Green's Yard owned by Thomas Green of Payne's Yard and occupied by Arthur Hillyard and James Hillyard

- six houses in Chapel Yard owned by Fred Tailby and occupied by Victor Rook, Tom Moore, Alfred Smith, John George, Arnold Webb and Charles Rook

- three houses in Kiln Yard owned by Patricia Eykyn and occupied by G A Ladkin, Samuel Measham and William Newcomb

- three houses owned by Lilian Eykyn of the Dower House and occupied by George Jacobs, William Moore and Josiah Fisher

- two houses in Banbury Lane owned by Mrs Waddell and occupied by William Keenes and Abraham Hannell.

People displaced

It was not until 6 December 1937 that these houses were closed, displacing 73 people. W R Keenes, J E Hillyer, J Hillyard, J T Jacobs, John (Jack) George, A Barker, R W Moore and A E Hefford moved into eight new council houses in New Road (Hillcrest Road). Fortunately many of the old cottages were not demolished until much later and so they were able to house evacuees from London during the second world war.

Hillcrest Road houses had running water

The houses were built, through representation by the Parish Council, with piped cold water. What a treat that must have been! Nonetheless, to have a hot bath, water had to be heated in a copper before being transferred to the bath. By contrast Brittains Cottages did not have a water supply brought into the kitchen until January 1960, two and a half decades later.

Changing times

The look of the village changed dramatically. Towcester Rural District Council's housing policy resulted in a total of 29 pre-war and war-time council houses being built in Gayton. In addition the first post-war house in Northamptonshire was completed at Gayton, a Swedish timber type semi-detached on the Bugbrooke Road, into which, on 6 July 1946 R A Green, an electrical wireman, and G Beveridge, a council surveyor, moved. By 1 July 1950, 14 post-war houses had been built with a further six in the course of construction.

Jack George on the steps of his brand new home in Hillcrest Road c1937

Corner Cottage

In the mid-1800s, a cooper, Saul Saull and his family rented Corner Cottage from Daniel Hart who also owned 1 High Street, next door. Throughout the majority of the nineteenth century the Saull's home was the only dwelling on the Bugbrooke Road which explains why it was known as Saull's Lane. Development of this part of the village began with the building of Glebe Farmhouse and, in 1901, the school. Miss Dora Parr MBE moved into Corner Cottage and from 1947 until her death on 9 February 1969 she was an active member of the village. Miss Parr encouraged Gayton WI to take part in amateur dramatics.

Corner Cottage c1908

Jane Almond, a later occupant of Corner Cottage was successful in arranging village fundraising events. One of the most notable was for Children in Need which raised over £1000.

Eastcote Road

Number 2 Eastcote Road was a very small thatched dwelling, just two rooms up and down, which had an outside privy. Outside the front door, in the centre of the cottage, was a traditional cobbled path. The cottage walls were substantial, 18 inches thick, and held together with lime mortar. The water supply was from two wells, one on either side. A chicken run was later built over to provide a kitchen, and a pig sty was replaced by a garage. The original staircase and two inglenooks are still in use.

Joseph Pettifer
Joseph Pettifer's first wife Mary (née Haynes) died, and he married Mary Yarlot in 1809. The 1802 date stone on the cottage probably records a major restoration of an existing hovel by Joseph. Mary continued living in the cottage after his death in 1827. On Mary's death in 1843 her son John sold the cottage to Thomas Payne for £18.

Mr Bolton with Mrs Coles outside 2 Eastcote Road c1896

Thomas Payne
Thomas Payne rented out the Pettifer's cottage, and when he retired from farming at the manor, built a brick house next door, East View Villa. In his will he left his housekeeper, Caroline 'Carrie' Wooton, furniture, wines, pictures, wearing apparel, linen and household utensils. Caroline was a local girl, who lived, and probably helped, at the Anchor Inn with her parents, James Ayers and Jane Wooton. Later she worked as housekeeper to the two brothers, Thomas and James Payne, at the manor house. When Caroline Wootton died aged 79 years in 1921 Revd Stokes wrote that she was a lady who was loved by all.

2 Eastcote Road c1946

Modernisation

In 1925, perhaps as a result of the chip shop at 2, Eastcote Road burning down, the roof was converted to corrugated iron. A year later Miss Emma Webber bought it and lived there till her death. It was sold to Mrs Ada Rogers in 1947. The roof was then tiled, and because it was not possible to stand up straight the ceiling downstairs was raised by 6 inches. The cottage remained in the Rogers family and in 1981 was extended and modernised once more.

2, Eastcote Road in 1991, with East View Villa in the background

Brittains Cottages

These cottages were the successors to the eight old almshouses, called Little Brittain in 1851-61, and built by the parish to house the poor and destitute of Gayton. During the First World War, the church allowed Mr Sparrow from Blisworth, master of the last operational ironworks, to build four houses for his workers on church land. They were built on the understanding that the houses would belong to the church when the ironstone working was finished. Although solid, well built houses they lacked services and did not have running water until the 1960s. When the ironstone workings closed in 1921 the houses reverted to the church but Aubrey Shipperley the foreman was allowed to continue living there.

Brittains Cottages replaced eight almshouses run by the church for the worthy poor

Chain Walk

The three cottages in Chain Walk in 1952

When this property was owned by George Coleman in 1841 it was one small old cottage (the building closest to the road) joined to a row of outhouses. Between 1841-71 this was extended into two cottages. By 1871 Edmund West had retired from helping his mother run Wood Farm. Ironstone mining had taken over the land and he moved to one of the cottages in Chain Walk. In the next ten years the two cottages had been increased to three. By 1953 when Mrs Hancock lived in one of the cottages, Ted Cockerill and Harold Kingston lived in the other two.

Deans Row and Rabbit Row

The top two cottages, 1 and 3 Deans Row were owned by the Hawleys in 1841. With Beech House and the Dower House they are the oldest buildings left near Kiln Yard. The Eykyn family purchased 1 and 3 Deans Row to house their family gardener and chauffeur. When the gardener left, George Dixon moved back to Gayton and worked as the Eykyn's rent collector. When the estate was sold in 1957 Mr Goosey bought his cottage, no. 3, for £400.

Rabbit Row

This row of ten, small, ancient cottages, some of which were thatched, also included the Co-operative Stores. Mrs Harriet Dunckley, who was a dressmaker, ran this shop in 1890 and Miss Clara Chellingworth took over in 1894. When Rabbit Row was demolished, at the turn of the twentieth century, the rubble was used in the building of other village cottages.

Drawing of Rabbit Row in the late nineteenth century from the WI *Scrapbook* of 1953

Beech House and Post Office Row

The house which still survives today and is known as Beech House can be seen (B) on the John Darker Estate map c1791, (on page 51). The property was let to William Dunckley by the Darker family, and consisted of tenement, workshop, outhouse, yard and garden. The paddock, Hills Close, behind Beech House was let to George Butler. In the south hedge of Hills Close were five elm trees and in the hedge on the west side were four pollarded ash trees. The house was extended by the addition of a row of cottages some time between 1814 and 1848. The work was probably undertaken at the instigation of Dr Butler. An ash tree in the front garden of the cottage next door to Beech House was originally planted by Joseph Ratledge and was not felled until after 'Bel' Ratledge's death in 1953. The row originally had front gardens but these were taken up by the widening of the west end of the road, Deans Row, (which formerly may have been called Church Street). As with many of the other cottages they had pit toilets with a bucket, and dirt drains. Although gas and electricity had been installed the water came from a pump outside the cottages, and an upgrading of the standards meant that they needed considerable modernisation. It was simpler to demolish and build again. The cottages, with the exception of the one adjoining Beech House, were demolished after the Eykyn's sale in 1957 and two bungalows built on the site. The cottage adjoining Beech House was incorporated into the house c1968.

1 and 3 Deans Row (Tanglewood and Meadowsweet cottages)

Gayton House

When Gayton House was Newe House

In the early 1600s a significant house is mentioned in Gayton called Newe House. It may have been built as a dower house for the lords of the manor, the Tanfield family, and had a little land attached. It was rented by Bridget Burton, a widow, who also rented the three acre field on the 'north side over against the street door'. In about 1624, Dorothy Tanfield leased it to Thomas Samwell and he in turn sub-let it to Francis Catesbie, esquire, of Gayton for five and a half years. Francis was a member of the Catesby family who became notorious after Robert's involvement with the gunpowder plot.

Sold to Mathias Wheelowes, dyer of Northampton

Matthias Wheelowes was moving up in the world when he bought and moved into Newe House from a 'messuage' between that of John Fryer and Thomas Tarry. Robert Tanfield sold him this 'house, edifice, building, barns, stables, yards, orchards, gardens and backsides' in 1630 along with fields called Wright's Ground, Lippiatts, Pillowe Hill and Gayton Lounde, together with John Tarry's cottage, all for £1,910. It was a significant building. The Wheelowes family continued living in Gayton for another 30 years after Matthias' wife's death in 1652 and his own in 1654.

The Lockwoods move in

This family was probably the next to live in Newe House. In the Church, to the left of the altar, high on the wall, is a white marble memorial tablet to Richard Lockwood who was buried in the family vault in the nave of Gayton Church. It is unusual because it gives a detailed family history of the Lockwoods through two generations.

Richard Lockwood

Richard married Susanna Cutts, daughter of Edward Cutts of Arkesden Essex. They were both sufficiently well off to have had a marriage contract to safeguard their interests. Richard Lockwood lived in Gayton but had a mortgage on Dews Hall, Essex and his son and heir, Richard junior, retired there in 1735 in order to live near his mother's family's seat. Richard senior also had a home in Newgate Street, London. He was a merchant, a financially hazardous occupation but he was lucky and became wealthy. In 1695 Northampton selected him as High Sheriff. He was a good man with a social conscience and left money in his will to place five child apprentices and also money for the poor of Gayton, Tiffield, Northampton and Towcester.

Mr Hartley

The trail of Newe House can be picked up again when a certain Mr Hartley died and his estate was sold to Richard Kent senior. Richard Kent split the Hartley property into two lots. He kept the house as his residence with part of the land creating a smaller estate worth around £300 or £400 at the time. The rest of the land was incorporated into the manor-house holdings on which he had a mortgage.

Richard Kent, fishmonger

The mortgage on the manor-house was an investment for Richard Kent and he could not afford to live there. Instead he chose to live in the 'smaller' Newe house which was eventually sold on to John Darker when Richard Kent junior died in 1780 (see 'A Long Time Ago').

John Darker Esquire, hop merchant

John Darker was born in Stoughton in Leicestershire and made a large fortune as a London hop merchant. He was treasurer of St Batholomew's Hospital and a fellow of both the Royal and Antiquarian Societies. As an MP at Westminster, he sat on trade and commerce committees because of his experience. He retired to his estate in Gayton.

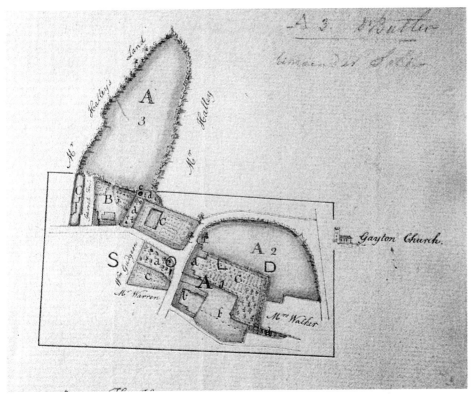

The first Gayton House is indicated by A1 on John Darker's Estate Map of 1791

Lavish entertainment

Four years after Darker's death in 1784 his 'neat and genteel household furniture' was sold by auction. The size and scale of the entertaining he had enjoyed in Gayton can be glimpsed from his 'fifty lots of china' which included 'a table service of fine blue containing 112 pieces; a tea set of 46 pieces and a punch bowl of 22 gallons and a half'.

William Blake

John Darker's daughter, already a widow and heiress, married Edward Loveden-Loveden in 1785. The Darker estate devolved upon her son, William Blake. The old house had deteriorated to being a farmhouse occupied by Thomas Payne. The Rector of Gayton, Dr George Butler, purchased it, pulled it down and built a new mansion house on the site.

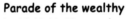

View of Deans Row drawn in 1848 by W G Butler. The carrier's cart can be seen at the far end of the road. The small building on the right-hand side is possibly the icehouse for Gayton House.

Parade of the wealthy

In 1841 Mr Kennard was left to fulfil the minister's role in Gayton while George Butler holidayed in Boulogne. Butler's daughter, Louisa, commented that Mr Kennard 'had scarcely then begun to be eccentric'! Revd George Kennard and his wife Mary Jeanette may have been the first tenants in the new Gayton House. A succession of the well-to-do rented the house, such as the Honourable William Booth Grey who died in 1852, and Richard Lee Bevan and his wife Isabella Judith Maria. When George Butler died in 1853 the property was sold to the sitting tenant, Charles Pilgrim MP. Henry Thomas Salmon JP bought the house in 1865 and sold it to Major John Stephenson Ferguson in 1872.

Roger Eykyn

Roger Eykyn's purchase of Gayton House was to mark the beginning of a new era for Gayton and the house. In 1874 he added bay windows and an entrance porch. Somewhere around this time the Squirrel Inn was removed from the corner of the Gayton House estate to the High Street.

Roger Eykyn

Gayton House c1900

View of Post Office Row and Rabbit Row from the roof of Gayton House c1900

Hissssss!

An insight into Eykyn's life was given twenty years later, in 1894, when Revd Arthur Gray Butler wrote to his sister that 'Eykyn is a tremendous Tory now and has taught his parrot to hiss Gladstone.'

Arthur Eykyn

When Roger Eykyn died he had no children so his estate passed in 1899, to the 36 year old Arthur Eykyn, who was the son of his brother Thomas. Arthur Eykyn bought and lived at the Dower House but after a very short time moved to Gayton House. He married Lilian Gertrude Pillar in 1902 and their son and heir, Roger, was born in 1904.

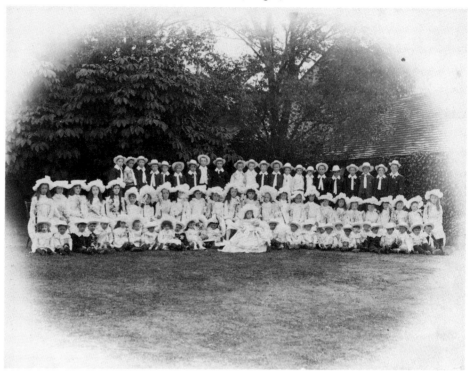

Gayton children, 22 July 1904, the day of the christening of Roger Eykyn, son of Arthur Eykyn

The maids downstairs

Many of the young girls from the village went into service. A few were lucky enough to work in one of the big houses in Gayton. Elsie Cockerill was the Eykyn's cook at Gayton House in the 1930s and Maggie West first worked at Gayton House and then moved to the Dower House, as did Nancy Paul who was an under parlour-maid to Mrs Eykyn.

No Noel for Nancy

Christmas was a very busy time for Nancy. No family celebrations for her, only a couple of hours snatched away from the hectic catering for Mrs Eykyn's large house-party. The evening before Christmas the front door would stand open and the bell ringers, choir boys,

The Dining Room at Gayton House set for a meal

Although not in service in her home village, Pem Folwell's uniform was typical of that worn in the big houses

Gayton House c1960

Scouts and Girl Guides would assemble to sing Christmas carols for their supper. On Christmas Day the long dining room table was carefully laid with silver cutlery and groaned with food. A huge turkey would be carved and served with cranberries. It was Nancy's job to wait at table. When the meal was over and the guests retired replete, she and the butler washed, dried and sharpened the knives. Carefully they polished, then put away all the precious tableware.

A crimson pall

Arthur Eykyn died in May 1923. His funeral at Gayton was quiet, but at his own request the coffin was covered with a crimson pall. The grave was covered with flowers. In January 1932 his only son, Roger, died of pneumonia aged 27. Mrs Eykyn lived at the Dower House and the final Eykyn interest in Gayton was auctioned off in 1953.

St Marys Court

In 1972 the Eykyn estate in Gayton was transformed into a cul-de-sac of 12 modern detached houses, seen here in 1990. The existing trees and stone walls were left, preserving the original estate's character.

St Mary's Church

An engraving published in the *European Magazine* in 1801. Compare the square 'decorated' windows in this picture with the pointed 'Early English' ones from the nineteenth-century restoration.

Gayton church and churchyard c1917

Spot the difference!

The changing church tower, top left in 1901, top right after 1908 and bottom right as it appeared in 1981

Saxon beginnings

Gayton church has not always looked as it does today. The triangular Anglo-Saxon doorway in the tower indicates that there was a church here before the Norman Conquest. This is supported by the Domesday entry listing a priest as one of the inhabitants of the unnamed holding of Sigar de Chocques. Although it was built to serve the spiritual needs of the village, it would have been a small church suiting the size of the community.

Church and village growing together

The growth of the church reflected the development of the village. As with houses, when owners are well off they build extensions and when times are hard they spend only on necessities. The village population grew and aisles were added to accommodate the congregation and possibly village events such as a village fair. The roof of the church was lifted and windows put in to give more light. A porch was added as this gave a church status and a place for legal undertakings. On 1 May 1609 Edward Robins granted James Marks a mortgage on a haybarn and cowhouse. However Robins could reclaim the property if the money was not paid within 20 days of the 1 May 1616 in the Gayton church porch. In 1726 there was a great building project organised by William Ball the Churchwarden and William Gibbs the Rector. The tower was raised, strengthened and more bells were hung.

Inside the church

In medieval times the church interior was divided into two halves by a carved, wooden rood screen; the chancel and altar for the clergy, and the nave for the villagers. The screen's stone base is still evident in the church but the thirteenth-century original is now in the vestry. It would have been painted and gilded with pictures of the saints. Across the top there was a wooden platform, called a rood loft, and in front of that a beam. On this beam, filling the top of the chancel arch, there would have been an enormous crucifix (the rood) with the figure of the Virgin Mary on one side and St John on the other.

From St George to St Mary the Virgin

In 1322 the church was dedicated to St George but by 1441 was re-dedicated to Our Lady. Church names were fashionable, and many churches were re-dedicated to St Mary. Gayton eventually settled on St Mary the Virgin. When people were dying their thoughts turned to God, and their wills often included references to the parish church. Between 1499, when Thomas Chapelen died, and 1528, when Jone Foster and Thomas Wapull died, the main altar of the church was dedicated to Our Lady and after 1516 was decorated with ornaments. There were also two other altars: one to St Nicholas with a statue of Mary next to it, and another dedicated to St Margaret for which J Lucas left money to buy candles.

A glow of candles

In 1510, T Farman left money for two candles to be burned in front of the crucifix in the rood, whilst J Hunt in 1516 left the income from two strikes (a bushel) of barley to the upkeep of the rood or for candles to be burned. The remains of a staircase and doorway leading to the missing rood loft can still be seen next to the pulpit. On festival days the screen would have be decked with foliage and candles lit. Soloists from the choir would have appeared high up in the loft to sing and the priest would have read parts of the service there, giving a dramatic effect.

The Church was restored by Dr George Butler 1826-8. This photograph of the east window was taken c1875.
The window was altered in 1883 by Revd John Clough Williams Ellis.

Chancel and east window from the nave after Revd John Clough Williams Ellis' restoration of 1883

Interior of church before 1953, looking towards the altar.
The Mothers' Union banner takes pride of place.

A choir stall carving

Looking from the chancel towards the west tower wall in 1994.
The marks of the steep-pitched old roof are clearly visible.

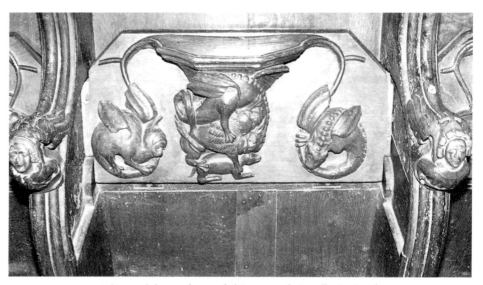

A lion and dragon forever fighting on a choir stall misericord

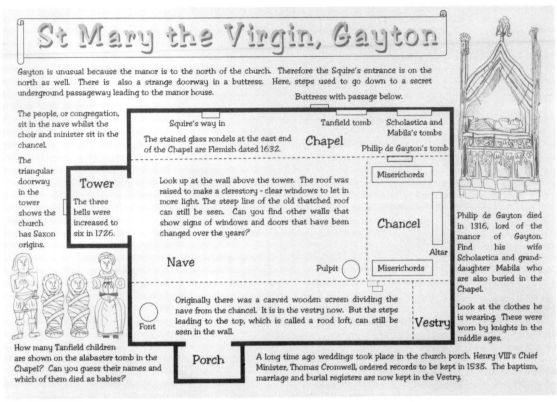

St Mary the Virgin, Gayton

Gayton is unusual because the manor is to the north of the church. Therefore the Squire's entrance is on the north as well. There is also a strange doorway in a buttress. Here, steps used to go down to a secret underground passageway leading to the manor house.

Buttress with passage below.

The people, or congregation, sit in the nave whilst the choir and minister sit in the chancel.

The triangular doorway in the tower shows the church has Saxon origins.

Squire's way in

The stained glass rondels at the east end of the Chapel are Flemish dated 1632.

Tanfield tomb

Scholastica and Mabila's tombs

Philip de Gayton's tomb

Chapel

Tower

The three bells were increased to six in 1726.

Look up at the wall above the tower. The roof was raised to make a clerestory - clear windows to let in more light. The steep line of the old thatched roof can still be seen. Can you find other walls that show signs of windows and doors that have been changed over the years?

Miserichords

Chancel

Altar

Nave

Pulpit

Miserichords

Originally there was a carved wooden screen dividing the nave from the chancel. It is in the vestry now. But the steps leading to the top, which is called a rood loft, can still be seen in the wall.

Font

Vestry

Philip de Gayton died in 1316, lord of the manor of Gayton. Find his wife Scholastica and granddaughter Mabila who are also buried in the Chapel.

Look at the clothes he is wearing. These were worn by knights in the middle ages.

How many Tanfield children are shown on the alabaster tomb in the Chapel? Can you guess their names and which of them died as babies?

Porch

A long time ago weddings took place in the church porch. Henry VIII's Chief Minister, Thomas Cromwell, ordered records to be kept in 1538. The baptism, marriage and burial registers are now kept in the Vestry.

Church Guide for children produced by Rita Poxon in 1998

Two Persian candlesticks were presented by Mr and Mrs Wright in memory of their son who was killed in an accident. They can be seen in this 1994 photograph, either side of the altar, on purpose built oak stands, commissioned by the Church Council.

The first Church Flower Festival on Friday 2 July 1982

Left to right:

Front row Viv Bailey, Josephine Chiswell, Gwen Crossley, Hazel Cohen and son Andrew

Back row Miss Lucas, Gwen Webb, Christine Webb, Phyllis Cokayne, Stephanie Platt, Mary Nightingale (further forward), Jane Patterson, Judith Gilbert, Celia Judge, Edith Cokayne, Joan Jeffery and son, Dan, Hilda Rook, Betty East and Joan McCarthy

Be good or else...

In some churches a backdrop was placed behind the crucifix in the rood loft as light from the east window made it difficult for the congregation to see it. This would be decorated with stars. Either side of the chancel arch the walls would be painted with a dramatic judgement scene, with everything from Christ and his angels, to the damned being prodded into a fiery hell by fiends with pitchforks. This was a graphic reminder to the mainly illiterate congregation of what was to come. The people were frightened of God and they needed reassuring saints through whom they could appeal to Him. Statues of St Catherine and St Mary Magdalene stood in the church. T Smythe in 1527 left money raised from two strikes of barley to the three saints, Catherine, Margaret and Mary Magdalene.

Compare this photograph of the churchyard in 1998. Notice how many of the gravestones from earlier centuries are still standing.

The church after Dr Butler's restoration, 1826-8, but before the vestry was added

More than old bones

As can be seen from the lack of gravestones in the early etchings of Gayton church, the majority of gravestones date from the 1800s. Gravestones can reveal secrets about people. A few headstones, like that of George Dunckley, give a potted history of the man, but more than that, of the community. He was 'clerk of this parish for 23 years; commencing that office in 1832'.

Well travelled people

Gravestones also indicate that travel was surprisingly common bearing in mind how slow and uncomfortable it was. Captain Cecil Eykyn died in the Boer War in 1900 at a village called Koodoosberg, in South Africa. Ann Hall, daughter of Edward and Mary Phipps who ran the Anchor Inn at the Banbury Crossing, died in Stonehouse (just outside Stroud) in Gloucestershire, whilst Mary Ann Jones, daughter of William and Ann George 'departed this life at Exeter, Devonshire' in 1845.

Immigrants

Thomas Coles was born in Wellingborough in 1815, and in 1822, Henry Claypole was born in Dundalk, just north of Dublin, but both settled and were buried in Gayton.

The churchyard before 1953

Victorian verse

Although quotations from the Bible were often added at the foot of the gravestone, poems sometimes replaced them. These were chosen primarily to point out a moral to the reader or to emphasize the circumstances of the deceased. In general the poems are lightly engraved and difficult to decipher; they use a traditional form of vocabulary and consist of one verse, or at most two, of four rhyming lines. They are fascinating and can tell us details we would have no other means of knowing.

Elizabeth George, daughter of William and Ann George, died aged 11 years in 1820:

> Within this grave here lies entombed
> A blossom cropt just as it bloomed
> So soon on earth the sweets decay
> The fairest flowers - thus fade away!

Robert Eason was accidentally killed in 1836 on the London and Birmingham Railway. He was only 23 years old:

> Death little warning to me gave,
> But quickly sent me to the grave,
> Repent in time, make no delay,
> For no-one knows their dying day.

Alice, wife of James Payne, died in 1820 and her husband must have been the one to choose this verse:

> Impartial fate to different ages sends
> His strict command to part the dearest friends
> I lost a loving wife, it is well known,
> And from her off-spring dear, a mother's gone -
> She's gone, alas, whose death we all lament
> But death's a blessing - to a life well spent.

Reminders of how tough life was, creep into these tributes, as with that of Elizabeth Cockerill who died in 1821 only 38 years old:

> From pain exempt, from wordly care
> I rest serene sleeping here
> With child-bed pangs oppress'd no more
> I'm landed on a peaceful shore
> Four children small there's left behind
> Also my husband - ever kind.
> Whene'er my friends, those children see,
> O! may they kindly think of me.

Very few poems try to console the reader, as this one inscribed at the bottom of the headstone dedicated to John Moore, the carrier operating from 1 High Street, and his wife Elizabeth, who ran the shop. They both died in 1875:

> Oh! weep not for the blessed dead,
> Nor wish them here again
> What! bring them back to earth and sin
> to feel its grief and pain.

Parish Priests

?	RALPH
1234	WILLIAM de ALBINIACO
1240	HENRY de CAMBREY, Sub-Deacon
1269	MICHAEL de NORTHAMPTON
1274	PHILIP de NORTHAMPTON, Sub-Deacon
1284	RICHARD de MEDEBURN, Chaplain
1304	WILLIAM de GAYTON, Accolyte
1342	SIMON de VEER, Clerk
1369	JOHN de HALDENBY
1370	JOHN, son of JOHN CURTEYS de JAKESLE
1373	WILLIAM BURGEYS, Chaplain
1396	WILLIAM PAUPAS
1401	HUGH PARKER, Chaplain
1408	JOHN ANDE, Priest
1421	JOHN VARNEY
?	RICHARD FEIRMAN
1471	THOMAS TANFIELD, DD
1472	THOMAS RUSSELL
1474	JOHN GRENBURGH
1475	THOMAS MAN
1505	RICHARD TOMLYNSON
1535	THOMAS GARDYNER

JOHN MILLYS, Rector 1544-80

John Millys was Rector of Gayton at a difficult time. His problems were summed up much later by Revd Marshall: 'He saw the changes under Henry VIII, the new prayer books of Edward VI, the reversion to Latin service books under Mary, and the return of the purified Catholic Faith under Elizabeth. It is not that there were different churches under these sovereigns, the Church of Rome and the Church of England - but it was the same Faith and the same Church and the same Rector; sometimes in union with Rome and sometimes not.' John Millys started the Gayton parish register in 1544. Unfortunately it was kept on paper which very soon started deteriorating.

JOHN MARKES, Rector 1583-1633

In 1597 John Markes had the earlier registers copied into a parchment book, as the Provisional Constitution of Canterbury required him to do. The entries date from 1558 and were approved by J Tanfield. John Markes was a wealthy man and supplied the land that provided for the Church Charity. His status was reflected in the fact that he was included in the 1612 Musters. Only the very well off had, like 'Mr Markes of Geaton', to provide 'Half Lighte Horses' for the defence of the realm. He was Rector during Gayton's enclosure and was buried on 17 March 1634, aged 81.

WILLIAM BURKITT BD, Rector 1633
William Burkitt had been Pattishall's vicar for six years when he took over the care of Gayton. From 1636-45 he was also vicar of Guilsborough.

RICHARD GIFFORD, Rector 1649-55
After the Dissolution of the monasteries Nicholas Gifford was granted St James' Abbey in Northampton. Richard Gifford was his grandson and was therfore able to acquire misericords from the dissolved St James' Abbey for Gayton Church. These beautifully carved seats had provided the abbey clergy with support when standing through long services. Second-hand they might have been, but for Gayton Church they were a wonderful treasure. Richard Gifford was buried on 2 March 1656 and Gayton was left without a Rector until 1662.

EDMUND MORGAN DD, Rector 1662-81
Edmund Morgan graduated from Magdalene Hall, Oxford. He was instigated in June 1662 by the bishop as the Samwells had made no appointment and Gayton had been without a Rector for seven years. He was buried at Kingsthorpe 11 February 1681, aged 67.

WILLIAM GIBBS, Rector 1682-1716
In William Gibbs time the people of Gayton enjoyed village events and fairs in the church or churchyard. Raising funds was always a problem for the church and they made money by brewing for church ales. These were very popular in the villages and profitable, too. However, they were frowned on by some who looked askance at the rise in population nine months later. Revd Gibbs owned a malt mill, barley and other paraphernalia for brewing.

WILLIAM GIBBS JNR, Rector 1716-41
Perhaps Revd William Gibbs junior inherited his father's brewing equipment, as during his time the church in Gayton undertook a great building project. In 1727, the tower of the church was raised, strengthened and the number of church bells increased to six, one being donated by Thomas Samwell. Thomas Wilson had the responsibility of carrying the bells to Gloucester and back. As with most arrangements, it was celebrated by drinking ale as the churchwarden's accounts record '...5 shillings for ale when they went to meet the bells at Fosters Booth and 4 shillings for ale when they got home...'.

JOHN THOMPSON, Rector 1741-53
John Thompson, graduate of Magdalene College, Cambridge, died in 1753.

WALTER GRIFFITHS, Rector 1753-92
Richard Kent bought the manor in 1753 with the right to present the Rector. Richard Kent was a tradesman who had made a lot of money. However, the local well-to-do disliked the brash manner of the 'nouveau riche'. George Tymms of Hartwell deplored the way in which the advowson at Gayton was 'most shamefully put up to a sort of auction'. The result was that Gayton received a young and wealthy incumbent in Walter Griffiths who had bought his living quite openly. Immediately Revd Griffiths installed a curate, John Jephcott, to do the work, probably for a low wage. Walter Griffiths died in 1792 leaving an estate worth approximately £5,000.

CHRISTOPHER HUNTER, Rector 1797-1814

In 1765 James Hawley sold the advowson to Sidney Sussex College, Cambridge for £1,400. Christopher Hunter was the first vicar of Gayton who was not dependent on the lord of the manor for his job. He was chosen from the College as he was the oldest available bachelor. From now on the ministers would be highly educated men.

GEORGE BUTLER, Headmaster of Harrow and Rector 1814-53

Born in London, 5 July 1774, and educated at his father's school in Chelsea, Butler went to Sidney Sussex College, Cambridge where he excelled at mathematics and classical studies. He became Rector of Calverton, Buckinghamshire (1814-21). He was Chancellor of Peterborough(1836-42) and Dean of Peterborough from 1842 until his death, 30 April 1853. He received the medal of the Royal Humane Society for leaping into the freezing canal near Gayton, aged 69, on a January day in 1843 to rescue a woman from drowning.

George Butler

Father of ten children

At 40 years old he was already Headmaster of Harrow School (1805-29) when he moved into Gayton Rectory. His father, Weedon Butler, became curate. On 18 March 1818 George Butler married Sarah Maria Gray, daughter of John Gray of Wembley Park, Middlesex. George Butler was a kind and loving father of ten children. He made sure the girls had a good education as well as the boys and they all went on to become influential people.

First the Church...

Butler had a profound effect on the church and an even greater one on the village. For example, the minstrels were disrupting the services by each playing in his own style and tempo. Knowing this would be an awkward problem to solve, Butler called a Vestry meeting. Since the difficult members of the Vestry were regularly late for meetings he rushed through an agreement to demolish the minstrel gallery. Workmen were standing by and had completed the work before the latecomers arrived. Perhaps to make amends Butler donated 'a neat organ' to replace the minstrels and then proceeded with his restoration of the church.

...then the Rectory

Butler embarked on several building projects in Gayton, but he started by enlarging the Rectory to house his family satisfactorily and to enable him to entertain. He spent £5,000 of his own money. Although rebuilt about 20 years earlier by Christopher Hunter, the previous incumbent, it was probably a little on the small side for Butler who was a well travelled man and a great scholar who did much entertaining. As a headmaster of a public school he had a wide circle of educated and influential friends.

...later Gayton House and a school

Dr Butler's distinguished presence lured many aristocrats and scholars to the country. He rebuilt Gayton House, which was then rented by a succession of wealthy gentry. Both Butler and his father believed deeply in the value of education, even for the poor. He instigated the building of a school for the village children although the lord of the manor, Hawley, refused to contribute. Improvements at the Dower House, once called the Deanery, are attributed to George Butler. When he died he owned a substantial amount of land and many houses in Gayton.

NICHOLAS JOHN TEMPLE, Rector 1853-76

Revd Temple had a difficult job to live up to the previous incumbent and appointed his stepson, John Whitehurst, as his curate.

JOHN CLOUGH WILLIAMS ELLIS, Rector 1876-89

Williams Ellis was born in Brondanw, Llanfrothen, Wales. Like his predecessors he made 'improvements' to the rectory and church and had Glebe farmhouse built. He was responsible for the rectory being re-roofed and having bow windows added. He also enlarged the graveyard. However, he left his successor many debts. His curate in 1883 was a member of the Eykyn family. Revd T Eykyn painted the signboard himself for the Crown and Squirrel pub.

The porch at Wendover records Revd J C W Ellis' restoration of the old Rectory in 1877

The gates to Gayton House are reputed to have been designed by Revd Williams Ellis' son, Clough. He was born on 28 May 1883 and lived until he was six years old at the Rectory. He become an architect famous for Portmerion which featured in a popular television programme, *The Prisoner*.

EDWARD GEORGE KING DD, Rector 1889-1920

Dr King was a Fellow of Sidney Sussex College, Cambridge. He was a distinguished scholar and an eminent authority on Greek and Hebrew religious works. He was also related to Dr Butler, a previous Rector. Dr King and his wife had three daughters, one of whom died when still a baby, and four sons, two of whom were killed during the war. His son, Hugh, before joining the 7th Northants in the First World War, was offered a job tutoring Count Tisza's sons in Austria. He declined, and later was relieved that he had done so, as the tutor who took the job became a prisoner of war. At the end of war by way of celebration for the returning soldiers, Gayton held a tea and sports. A brass band played and headed a procession around the village.

Dr King and the Methodists

Dr King had problems with the villagers leaving the Church of England and turning to Methodism. On a return visit to Gayton to preach, one of Dr Butler's sons, Revd Arthur Butler, commented on how dissent was splitting the village. He found it a difficult subject as he felt it sounded as if he was comparing his father's time with Dr King's. However, Dr Butler had had a problem with dissent himself. But in his day it was with people wishing to become Baptists. The chapel that first served the Baptists and then the Wesleyan Methodists, was built when Dr Butler was promoted to Dean of Peterborough and not able to concentrate on what was happening in Gayton. In both cases the rise of Nonconformism was only temporary. Wesleyan numbers declined c1908 and Dr King had a full congregation.

Beards, cars and biers

At the turn of the century there was a revolution in transport with the arrival of the motor car. Dr King's vehicle was the first in Gayton. The car was open topped, so when it rained both he and Mr Raymond, his chauffeur-gardener, who each had 'fine beards', put them in little sponge bags to keep them dry! Perhaps driven to compete with the Rector, the village started a fund to provide rubber tyres for the parish bier! They cost £10 and the money was raised from Whist Drives.

Sad loss

Dr King, died suddenly aged 76, on 8 February 1920. The parish was sad to lose the Rector and the Sexton, John Blunt, who had worked together for 30 years and who died within two weeks of one another.

WILLIAM FREDERICK STOKES, Rector 1920-33

Revd Stokes had been a master at Rugby School. One of his first duties in Gayton was to dedicate the First World War Memorial Tablet, made of Hopton-wood marble, on the last Sunday in September 1920. Captain, the Revd King, the son of the late Rector, performed the unveiling ceremony. This was to be the first visit of many, as Revd King's children kept close ties with the place where they had grown up, and returned frequently.

Revd Stokes hosted many charity events in the Rectory garden.
They did not always enjoy the good weather like this.

Dr King on the rectory lawn c.1920.
The mature trees date back to Dr Butler's time.

Dr King

Dr King's family

A new team of parish bell ringers

Bell ringing became popular with this generation in the 1920s. Revd Stokes was responsible for the recasting of the cracked fourth bell. At the same time John Taylor and Company's bell foundry rehung the peal of six bells with entirely new and modern fittings in a cast-iron framework on a foundation of heavy rolled steel girders. The work took four months during which time the clock did not strike and a single bell was hung temporarily for summons to service. The service of dedication took place on Saturday, 30 January 1932 conducted by the Rural Dean, Revd Canon W Bartlett, whose blessing was requested, as follows:

Mr Rural Dean, we the Rector, Churchwardens, Bellringers, Sidesmen and Parishioners of the Parish of Gayton in the Diocese of Peterborough do make our humble petition that you will be pleased to consecrate, hallow and set aside from all secular and profane uses, the bell that has been newly cast, and re-open for use the five other bells which have now been returned and rehung. All these bells are of interest, in that for over two hundred years they have called the faithful of the village of Gayton to the worship and praise of God. They will commence to-day with your blessing a new era of service for the successors of those to whom we believe they did not call in vain in times past.

Handbell ringers outside the church

Traditions grew of ringing the bells on 21 December, the King's birthday, on the shortest day, and at midnight on Christmas Eve. A muffled peal was rung for Queen Victoria's death and also on the Sunday after William Kingston, one of Gayton's oldest bellringers died, in his memory. The Oxford Diocesan Guild of Church Bellringers rang a true and complete peal of Bob Minor consisting of 5040 changes, in three hours and six minutes. Mr W A Ratledge, the Rector's Churchwarden, worked hard to raise the money to pay off the debt for repairing the bells. However, in 1934 this still stood at £56. The parish also owned a set of handbells with which the ringers entertained the village people.

Ascension Day was a holiday from school
The children's day off from school was spent preparing their flowers and gifts for the Ascension service. At 3pm the school children met the choir at the Church door and during a processional hymn they gave their tributes to the Churchwardens who handed them to the Rector to present at the altar. In Dr King's day the offerings were quite exotic; as well as eggs there were oranges, bananas, and asparagus. Revd Stokes' incumbency was dogged by inclement weather and sometimes the children had to have tea indoors and leave without 'the games and fun in the sunshine' in the Rectory garden. The village carrier, Charlie Simpson, who lived in Kiln Yard and provided the only transport for the village, took the Ascension gifts to Northampton hospital, free of carriage.

Money, money, money
Nothing changes! One thing came after another. The cross on the east end roof was damaged in the storms and had to be repaired, whilst the churchyard wall needed extensive repairs. The heating apparatus badly needed renewing but had to be left. Revd Stokes retired from Gayton in 1933. He settled with his family at Princes Risborough, Buckinghamshire. On 1 January 1945 he died and a memorial service was held in Gayton to coincide with the exact time of his funeral.

REVD HENRY MARSHALL, Rector 1933-35
Revd Marshall, in the short time he was in Gayton, made a real effort to get to know about the history of the village and church. He was well regarded for his charm and his way with words. In December 1934 he told the village, 'We have tried to give every house a Calendar for 1935 in the hope that each of the 365 days will be a day of blessings'. He suffered the usual financial troubles. The bell debt still was not paid, the heating in the church required attention, as did the organ and he could not see the diocesan obligations being fulfilled. To make this clear he included in the parish magazine a break down of how the money was being allocated. Henry Marshall was buried in Gayton churchyard on 13 February 1935.

LAURENCE E BROWNE, Rector 1935-46
Revd Browne was born in Northampton. His grandfather had been the first Vicar of St Edmund's whilst his father was a well known solicitor, E Montague Browne. Dr Browne was educated at Magdalen College School, Brackley and had served most of his ministry overseas in India. When he came to Gayton in 1935, he was a widower with a little boy and girl.

Vera Coulson, later Mrs Harry George, worked as a nanny for Revd Browne's children

The wedding of Dr L E Browne and Margaret Carpenter of Cold Higham, 8 August 1938. The eldest bridesmaid is Rosemary Barrow. The children are, from left to right, Peter Dickens, Ann Carpenter, Diana Dickens and Eric Dickens.

An aerial view of the church and the old rectory c1951. The churchyard wall was taken down to extend the churchyard.

Chasing butterflies

Vera Coulson became Nanny to the children and took care of them while Revd Browne and his wife Monica had a few days on their own in North Wales. It rained frequently but they visited the beauty spots and took butterfly nets with them. Catching butterflies was a popular past-time but the heavy rain spoiled their sport.

All warm and cosy at 60°F

Revd Browne's immediate concern was how cold the church was and in August 1936 work on the heating system started. It was turned on for the first time on 4 October 1936. Revd Browne reported that, 'An even temperature of 60°F in all parts of the church is easily obtained, without smell or stuffiness. Nothing is visible except the one grating, flush with the floor near the vestry. Our thanks are due to Messrs Chase and Co., the manufacturers of the McClary Pipeless Heaters, Messrs Edward Green and Son of Northampton who did the builders' work and our organist, Mr Anderson who installed electric light in the crypt.' The cost was £240. However, this was fully paid by February 1944.

The Revd Professor

In 1941 Browne was appointed Professor of Comparative Religion at Manchester University but he continued with his duties at Gayton. VE Day in 1945 was celebrated with a short informal service at 8pm and a bonfire and torchlight procession round the village. Laurence E Browne left Gayton in March 1946.

IVAN MAVOR, Rector 1946-51

Revd Mavor was previously a master at St Paul's School. When he joined Gayton, the large Rectory was in a dilapidated state. Poorly maintained rectories were a national problem, as for many years rectors had not been paid sufficiently well to look after these rather grand houses. Finally the church and the council agreed to the selling of the Old Rectory and the building of another.

Let there be light

In 1947, once the war blackout was no longer a problem, higher powered lamps were put in the church and the lights at the gates were repaired. In addition, chairs for the Lady Chapel were ordered so that it could be used for meetings. In 1949 the church roof had to be repaired costing £1000, half of which had to be borrowed. The firm of Norman and Underwood undertook the work. The churchyard needed to be extended and a quarter of an acre was added to the east end. The first burial in the new part of the churchyard, that of Anna Elizabeth Sturgess aged 74, was conducted on 29 August 1951.

WILLIAM HENRY OLIVER, Rector 1952-56, and Rector of Tiffield

On the financial front, a fund was started for a processional cross. The organ needed renovating and the work was given to Starmer Shaw and Son and cost £300. Mr George Dixon made a sliding shutter with two keys to lock up the organ blower and also a book rest. Finally a gift of £150 from the Church Extension Board paid off the outstanding debt for the church roof.

Revd Oliver officiating at the wedding of Olive Folwell and
Ron Brown on 22 March 1952

The new Rectory

Revd Oliver was made Curate-in-Charge and Rector designate
while the accommodation problem was resolved. He explained to
the congregation that the new Rectory was larger than he, a
celibate, required, but it had to be large enough to cater for a
Rector's family in the future.

Girls became choristers c1958

Left to right:
Back row   Sheila Cokayne, 'Pem' Folwell and Gladys White
Front row   Sandra Jacobs, Avis Bevan, Rosemary Bryan, Linda Ratledge, and Blodwyn Bevan

Girl Choristers

Following the war, society had changed and congregations were falling. There was a muffled peal of six bells for a Remembrance Service when the Rector noted that 60 men came to church. Another sign of the changing times was that the sum of £2 10s was recorded as being lost in a robbery. Women's attitudes were changing, too. With Miss Parr's generous donation, six girls were able to become fully robed choristers. Three years later square hats in the same material as their gowns, and made by Mesdames Hildred, Markham, Marston and Misses Lansley and Parr, were introduced as part of the choir girls' outfits. When he left Gayton, his last service being 8 July 1956, Revd Oliver left his cope and other vestments as his personal gift to the parish.

HENRY JOHN WELLER, Rector of Gayton with Tiffield 1956-65

Although Henry Weller was not known in Gayton when he became Rector, he had many friends who had close ties with the village. He had worked with Revd King's son Hugh, and was a friend of Dr L E Browne.

ERNEST GEORGE ORLAND, Rector of Gayton with Tiffield 1965-69

Revd Orland was 41 when he came to Gayton, married with two young children. He was born at Long Buckby. Having served an apprenticeship at the British Thompson Houston works, he became an engineering draughtsman there until 1960. He then trained for the ministry at the Lichfield Theological College. He was a keen bellringer and president of the Peterborough Diocesan Guild of Church Bellringers. He also played cricket.

CANON DENIS BROWN, Rector of Gayton with Tiffield 1970-89

'How you doing, Rector?' Canon Brown is remembered by many people in Gayton for his cheery riposte, 'Still avoiding the undertaker'. He was a man who had spent an eventful life. He was ordained in 1937 and worked in Newcastle until he was sent to Borneo as a missionary priest. His stories of his days during the war in a Japanese prison camp were most distressing. Food was scarce for the prisoners and their diet would be supplemented by a large variety of wild life, from crawling insects to snakes.

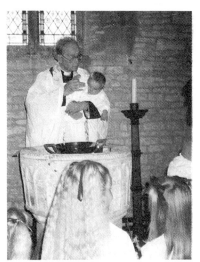

Canon Brown christening Claire Ratledge, daughter of Mark and Jacky, in 1987

Red Cross worker

Besides his pastoral work he had a great commitment to the Red Cross. His skills were called upon at many local events where he tended a wide variety of incidents. He became the deputy director of the Northampton branch in 1971 and was made a Knight of the Order of St Lazurus. He retired from the priesthood after 50 years service, 19 of them in Gayton, and he had served 32 years when he retired from the Red Cross. Married with two daughters, whilst in Gayton he suffered the loss of both his wife Marjorie, who died 21 March 1977, and his daughter, Gwen, who died 26 November 1984 aged only 34 years.

FATHER PAUL BROADBENT, Rector of the United Benefice of Gayton with Tiffield and Pattishall with Cold Higham 1991-

Today, the Rector lives in Pattishall and has four parishes in his benefice, Tiffield, Cold Higham, Gayton and Pattishall. He has all the same problems of deteriorating church buildings as did his predecessors, but multiplied by four! To celebrate the Millennium some parishioners trained to ring the bells thus maintaining a good Gayton tradition. Saturday morning practise meant that the bells rang out over the weekends leading up to New Year's Eve. On 1 January 2000 a short service was taken by Eric White, churchwarden, and attended by a large congregation to celebrate 2000 years from the birth of Jesus Christ, and to ring in the new millennium.

In May 2000 the alabaster Tanfield tomb was restored by David Carrington of the Skillington Workshop to ensure that it survives well into the century. Grants from the Council for the Care of Churches, the Manifold Trust and South Northamptonshire Council have enabled this work to be carried out.

Revd Paul Broadbent officiating at the wedding of Olivia Warren and Kevin Sparkes on 2 August 1997

Lady Palmer and Jane Pattison instigated a hassocks renewal project in February 1990 whereby people in the community sponsored a hassock. Over five years 192 hassocks were embroidered using 20 different designs. Pictured left is Rene Dundas working on a tapestry.

Chapel Life

Were they Quakers?

The gravestone in a Gayton back garden

The good news

How does a gravestone come to be in a back garden in Gayton? Well, there is good news and bad news. The good news is that it is well preserved and reads:

**HER LYETH THE
BODY OF IZABEL
HOPKINES WIFE
OF ROBERT
HOPKINES
WHO DIED THE
VI NOVEMBER
ano. d. 1681**

The bad news

The bad news is that we do not know why it is there. However in 1668 the following words were written in the parish register of nearby Bugbrooke:

'About this time that untoward Generation of Quakers began to bury theirs distinctly by themselves in their Gardens and Orchards in several places of the Towne'.

Perhaps, maybe, possibly

Although the Quakers were persecuted they did keep some records. From these records we know that the Hopkins family of Muscott were Quakers.

First clue
There is an account of a meeting at the home of Henry Hopkins on 23 August 1663 where there were 200-300 people present. A corporal and five soldiers with a Justice's warrant entered the meeting with pistols cocked. They took away eight people, amongst them William Lovel of Hardingstone, Joseph Gammage of Bugbrooke and Thomas Dent of Kislingbury. So people were present at Henry Hopkin's meeting from villages local to Gayton.

Second clue
Another account tells of a similar meeting in Bugbrooke on the 6 September 1663, from where William Hopkins, William Simpson and Richard Ashby were taken. It is not much to go on, but people called Hopkins were Quakers and they worshipped in Bugbrooke which is only a couple of miles from Gayton, and at the right time. Circumstantial evidence. Whatever the story behind Izabel Hopkines, her gravestone, although not in consecrated ground, is the oldest legible gravestone in Gayton!

The Baptists

Conflict between the Church of England and the Baptists
New forms of religious worship competed for congregations with the established church. It was not until George Butler was made Dean of Peterborough and was absent for long periods, that the Church of England lost its tight control on the Gayton people. Villagers became Baptists and built their own chapel as others in the villages round about were doing. But the church records were maintained by those in the Church of England. James McKee, Gayton's curate, states that in 1851 there were only three dissenting families in the village. A curious comment when a new Baptist Chapel had been built in Gayton only six years earlier.

Build me a Chapel
On 31 May 1845 Elizabeth Coleman, a well-to-do old lady living in Gayton, challenged Revd Thomas Marriott of Milton Malsor to build a Baptist Chapel on a piece of land 30 feet by 22 feet that she would make available. She also gave him £50 towards the building fund. Elizabeth Coleman was Thomas Coleman's widow and her son, also Thomas Coleman, had just died. She overcame her sad circumstances by giving herself a purpose. Now the Baptist congregation of Gayton and nearby could worship closer to home. The Chapel was built in the centre of a group of old cottages which were to become known as Chapel Yard.

Boots for Cromwell
The Church of England has never had an easy time in Northamptonshire. Northampton people have always been extremely sympathetic to other forms of Christianity. This was a trait which they demonstrated by supplying Cromwell with boots for his army and bringing the wrath of kings down upon their heads! As early as 1676, even the ministers of Roade

and Stoke Bruerne were acknowledging that there was support for other types of church worship in their villages and it is supposed that this dissenting religion came from nearby Newport Pagnell where John Gibbs (a friend of John Bunyan who wrote *The Pilgrim's Progress*) preached. A new Baptist meeting house was built at Roade in 1736, so by that date there must have been a sizeable congregation.

Kislingbury, Bugbrooke, Blisworth and Milton Malsor
Bugbooke in 1805 and Kislingbury in 1810 each built a Baptist chapel. Blisworth followed suit breaking away from Roade to form its own church on 7 October 1825. On 4 July 1841, Blisworth employed Revd John Goddard Stephens as pastor for the sum of £52 per year. Joseph Dent, a Baptist deacon from College Street Baptist church, Northampton encouraged the people of Milton Malsor to license a farmhouse to provide a meeting house until their chapel was built in 1827.

Milton Malsor Baptists license a meeting house in Gayton
In 1833 the Milton Baptists rented Mary Pell's cottage in Gayton and licensed it as a meeting house. Milton and Blisworth took it in turns to supply a preacher. Finally, on 31 May 1845 the Gayton congregation took steps to form their own church which they built on Elizabeth Coleman's land known as Garden Ground. Not long afterwards Gayton poached Blisworth's pastor John Stephens and he and his wife moved into the village. Mary Stephens ran a day school.

A Baptist Chapel and pastor for Gayton
The chapel was most definitely destined to have a chequered history. It was probably unfortunate that it was built towards the end of what was a period of expansion for the Baptist cause. It was quite large having 100 seats but it is difficult to imagine them ever being filled. The Baptist cause dwindled but the chapel remained open, even after Revd Stephens retired, until Elizabeth Coleman died, aged over 88. Mr Nicholas Fisher travelled to Gayton from Milton on a Sunday to preach to a congregation of sometimes only two people. The abandoned chapel started to deteriorate but this was not the end of its story.

The Wesleyan Methodists

The second-hand chapel
A small community of Methodists existed in Gayton, which included Benjamin and Mary King who had their child baptised in 1844. At this time they appear to have been using a building behind the Queen Victoria as a chapel. They took over the Baptist Chapel on 25 March 1880 at £2 *per annum,* although this was never formalised. A new floor and gallery were installed and the whole was redecorated. New lamps and stove were added. The repairs totalled £43 15s 9d. A split occurred within the Methodists at national level, and by 1907 the Gayton congregation had 'gone over' to the Wesleyan Reformers. About 12-18 people attended the services.

A new life

The chapel was a tall imposing building built of red brick. The entrance was from a door in the wall facing the direction of High Street and it had a window on either side. Inside the hall, just above the doorway, was a balcony that stretched across from one side to the other and was reached by an inside stairway. Opposite the door was a lectern, which was like a wooden cupboard with a sloping top, where the Bible would rest. The wooden pulpit to the left of the lectern was reached by two or three steps and very similar to the pulpit in the church. Services were held to the accompaniment of an old fashioned harmonium. The seating consisted of chairs and benches which were stained a deep red, which by the end of their life was peeling and discoloured.

Sitting in the balcony

Every Sunday a Methodist minister would travel to Gayton to take the service, and a Sunday School was opened. Everyone seems agreed that the highlight of the children's visit to the chapel was sitting upstairs in the balcony! The chapel held its Harvest Festival service on a Sunday and then, one evening the following week, sold off the produce. Mary Nightingale, when a child, went along and bought a marrow for a few pence. She remembers being delighted with her purchase and running home to show her mother.

The chapel entered a twilight world

By the beginning of the First World War the congregation had dropped to 20, and the Sunday School had closed. The chapel was now uncertain of its ownership or status due to the Baptists' bad management. They never made a legal agreement with the Methodists, probably grateful to be receiving £2 a year on a regular basis and relieved of the responsibility of a building that was decaying. However, when the Baptists became insolvent years later all the trustees were dead and there was no one legally available to put the Chapel up for sale. Before they could do anything they had to arrange new trustees.

In 1927 the Methodists gave up their struggle for survival

By the late 1920s, two members of the church had left Gayton and another died, leaving a congregation of two Gayton people aged 82 and 86 (one may have been Mrs Henry Clarke), Mr C Lucas and Miss Lucas who lived one mile out of Gayton. The last member of the congregation was Miss Grace Hillyard who was over 70 and lived in Dalscote, from where she had walked to church for the previous 24 years. She informed the Baptists that the Methodists were no longer willing to rent the chapel and that the man who owned the cottages around the chapel was interested in buying it. Nothing happened. It was not until 1938 that negotiations restarted. By then the chapel had deteriorated further and an order of demolition was put on the cottages. They were deemed unfit for human habitation and none of the parties wanted to buy. Again nothing happened.

Wartime affluence!

In 1941 the Baptists, again looking to sell the chapel, visited Gayton and found circumstances had changed drastically. Evacuees from East Ham were occupying the cottages and paying rent to the owner. They were using the tumbledown chapel for storage. In a letter to Towcester, the Baptist hierarchy suggested that the evacuees should be paying rent, whilst at the same time commenting on the 'deplorable' condition the chapel was in. They even suggested that perhaps the Baptists should be offering some 'religious influence'. After the war the evacuees left and in the 1950s the ruins of the chapel were demolished and Towcester Rural District Council built houses on the land.

Boy Scout Patrol takes over the old chapel

Robert Baden-Powell founded the Boy Scout movement in 1908 and three years later in November 1911, Mr Sidney Taylor from the Dower House started a patrol of Boy Scouts in Gayton. It was such a success that seven months later another patrol was formed and John Hillyer was elected leader with Geoffrey Chester as second in command. Mr John George volunteered to help and also donated one boy's complete outfit. In addition the project was supported financially by Gayton Alms Fund, Dr and Mrs King, and Mr T R Walker.

Miss Constance King ran the scouts c1915

Gayton won the Hanney Banner
By 1915 Miss Constance M King, the Rector's daughter, was Scoutmaster with John Hillyer, A Roberts and H Hillyard as Assistants. The Gayton scouts competed against Pattishall and Greens Norton and won the Hanney Banner. At this time the scout cabin was a building in Blisworth Road near the Rectory. In June 1916 a party of scouts from Far Cotton camped in Home Farm's barn and the Gayton scouts joined them for a parade service.

The Cubs, no offence!
In November 1931 a junior division was formed called cubs 'with no disparagement to the individuals' and soon afterwards Mrs Hawley started a Gayton branch of the Girl Guides, assisted by Ruth Crockett and Margaret Stokes.

Chapel serves as scout hut

In the late 1920s, John Hillyer had graduated to scoutmaster. The old chapel had been abandoned by the Methodists and still not reclaimed by the Baptists so he used the old chapel building as a scout hut until the war.

Gayton Scouts c1930

Left to right:
Back row	Terry Wright, Harold Kingston, Ernie Cockerill, Denis Cockerill, Bill Garrett George Paul
Middle row	Eric Ratledge, Eric Hillyer, John Hillyer, Harry George, Jack Kingston
Front row	Bob Moore, Ken East, Vic Measham, Charlie Jacobs, Reg Castle

Traycloth belonging to Black Cat patrol

Cooking over a camp fire with Scout Leader John Hillyer, right

Postcards from Gayton

'Cartomania'

Picture postcards were first produced and sold in the 1890s. By1900 there was a tremendous choice and people all over the country sent and collected postcards. Gayton was photographed from every angle as can be seen in the selection of postcards shown here and on the following pages.

S 4677. High Street, Gayton.

S 4679. High Street, Gayton.

S 4680. The Green, Gayton.

S 4678. High Street, Gayton.

S 4676. Deans Row, Gayton.

Now you see it...

...now you don't

St. Mary's Church, Gayton

GREETINGS FROM

GAYTON

Growing up in Gayton

Day schools and Sunday schools

The village children were taught from 1801 at the Sunday School under George Dunckley's supervision. For many of the poor this was their only schooling. In 1818 there was one Day School and one Sunday School in the village and by 1833 there were two Day Schools and one Sunday School. Day schools, in general, were the child minders of their day, giving little teaching.

SACRED
TO
THE MEMORY OF
GEORGE DUNCKLEY
MASTER OF THE SUNDAY SCHOOL
45 YEARS ENDING IN 1846;
AND CLERK OF THIS PARISH 23 YEARS;
COMMENCING THAT OFFICE IN 1832:
WHICH HE HELD
TILL THE TIME OF HIS DEATH
WHICH OCCURED SEPTR 27TH 1855:
AGED 80 YEARS

The Dunckley gravestone

Children taught children

Dr Butler's young family helped run the Sunday School. On Sunday morning the school was held in the Rectory laundry room. When this finished all the children joined the morning Service. After lunch, they returned for the afternoon Service and then Sunday School classes were held in church. It was not until after their six o'clock tea that the Rector's children were free for their own family activities.

How many people could read and write?

Communication by letters and newspapers depended on people having reading and writing skills. We know that Gayton children had the opportunity to attend a Sunday School as early as 1801. But were the village people literate before that? The *Northampton Mercury*, a local newspaper had been available from 1720, so there was a demand for local news. In small communities, someone would sit in the inn and read items from the newspapers to customers. Private letters, too, were read when it was required. It was customary for a person's will to be dictated to the priest when they were extremely ill. The words, 'sick in body but of a sound disposing mind' being used frequently.

Gayton National School

Gayton's first school was intended to educate the children of the poor in the principles of the Established Church, and accepted both infants and older children, boys and girls. A teacher's house was attached to it. Revd Butler employed a well known church architect, S S Teulon, to draw up the plans and supervise the work. Butler gave the land together with permission to dig stone for building out of pits on his private property but the ironstone quoins (cornerstones) were obtained from Duston quarry. A local man, Richard Dunckley, from Blisworth, started building on 25 June 1845. The work cost £260 1s 3d.

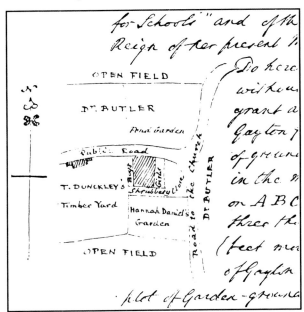

Butler's sketch showing land he gave for the school

Ten shillings to stand for the committee, five shillings to vote

Those making donations of ten shillings towards the school were eligible to both vote and stand as a member of the committee, but those making donations of five shillings were only eligible to vote. Mrs Kennard, Sir Joseph Hawley, the Dean of Peterborough (George Butler), Edward Rawnsley, Mrs Coles, Charles Mathews (through John Chamberlain), William Payne snr, James Payne jnr, William West, James Payne (through Walter George), Mrs Coleman, and W Higgins were all eligible to stand. In addition, John Chamberlain, William Payne jnr, Mrs West, William Harris and John West were eligible to vote. Roger Eykyn, Charles Smith, Master of Sidney Sussex College, Cambridge and the Rector, Revd King took over as trustees when all the original trustees had died.

Gayton National School Rules set by Dr Butler in 1846

1. That no Child be admitted having any infectious diseases or not having been vaccinated.
2. That the Children attend punctually at 9 in the morning and at 2 in the afternoon, washed, combed and clean.
3. That Two pence weekly be paid for each poor child, where one only of a family is admitted, and one penny weekly for every additional child of the family if there be more than one at a time. NB This is to be understood only of the children of the poor; the children of the richer inhabitants, Farmers and Tradespeople, are to pay sixpence a week each. The Sunday School Children to be taught gratuitously.
4. That each child bring his or her weekly pence every Monday morning at first school and be not admitted until the payment be made in advance for the week following. The children are not to be admitted without payment of the money.
5. That no occasional absence exempt any child from the payment of the weekly pence, accepting on a plea expressly sanctioned by the officiating Minister of the parish or by the Committee of Management.
6. That the Children be never detained at home or taken from the school without a satisfactory reason assigned by their parents or friends.
7. That the hours of attendance in School be from 9 till 12 in the morning and from 2 till 5 in the afternoon excepting in the winter months when the school will close at 4 o'clock.
8. That every Sunday the children of the school above six years of age be required to attend both morning and afternoon in the Sunday School and to proceed in an orderly manner two and two from School to Church and from Church to School. (Parents are particularly requested to hear their children daily repeat their Morning and Evening prayers and every Sunday the Collect of the day and their Church Catechism.)
9. That all applications for admission into the School be made to the Officiating Minister of the Parish.
10. That such children as do not strictly observe the above Rules be expelled from the School.
11. The weekly pence collected by the School Mistress every Monday morning are to be handed over by her to the Officiating Minister of the Parish who will take an early opportunity of depositing them in the savings bank at Northampton.

George Dixon became Head Teacher

The trials and tribulations of the school unfold in the search for a competent school teacher until finally Mr G E Dixon was appointed on 21 April 1862. He was to be headmaster for 36 years. His daughter, Carrie became assistant school mistress at 19. Her sister, Annie, took over from her in 1896. Annie resigned on 3 August 1906 as she was to be married to Mr William Radford Raymond of Worksop. Mrs Dixon held the reception in a marquee at the White House with over 50 guests. When the couple left for their honeymoon in the Isle of Man the school children lined the route carrying bundles of flowers.

National School's first Management Committee

The School Managers' Minute Book gives details of the history of the school from conception. It details the advantages of being established in union with the National Society with the names of local people who supported the project and how much they donated. The regulations for the annual meeting to be held on Easter Monday are given and the members of the Management Committee which were to consist of the Rector, the Curate, and four members of the Established Church.

Gayton National School Log Book

21 Oct 1898	20 children played truant to see Barnum and Bailey's Show in Northampton.
24 May 1899	Mr Dixon - Master resigned his post as Head Master.
25 Apr 1900	Ringworm is keeping three of the Infants from school.
4 May 1900	Closed for Club Holiday.
22 May 1900	Mr Usher HMI visited school to inquire about the progress of the proposed New School.
20 Mar 1901	An object lesson was given on the census. This lesson will be repeated before 1 April.
9 Jul 1901	No school today. Removed apparatus to New School. As no cupboards are fixed the books etc have to be arranged at present on the floor.
10 Jul 1901	Managers visited New School at 9 o'clock am and formally opened School with short Service of Prayers. Present. Revnd Dr and Mrs King, W George Esq, H W Wheldon Esq, E J Brown Esq.
9 Sep 1901	Re-opened School. Attendance fair. Admitted three new scholars (girls). The school is still in an unfinished state. Not sufficient cupboard room. Books etc still to be on the floor. School visited by Rev Dr and Mrs King also Mrs A Eykyn (Gayton House) and friends.

Gayton National School Log Book extracts which provide fascinating details of school life both at the little school in Deans Row and at the present school when it was brand new

The Old Schoolhouse in 1994 which has since been modernised

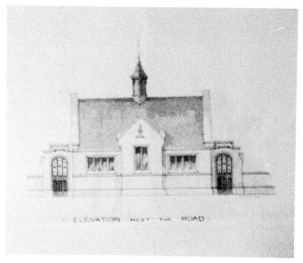

Water colour from Law's Plans of 1870

School children in front of the Old Schoolhouse c1870

The school in 1897 when Mr George E Dixon was headmaster 1862-99

From left to right:

Back row	Percy Plumeridge, Walter Hillyer, Reggie Hillyer, Ernest Kingston, Harry Heel, Tom Cockerill, Lucy Timson, Ruby Ratledge, Tom Henning, Charlia Simpson, Harold Kingstone
Second row	Teacher, Nellie Ratledge, Edith Green, Amy Hillyard, Maggie Timson, Elsie Hillyard, Bob Cowley, Tom Payne, Henry Dunckley, Teacher
Third row	Nellie Cockerill, Annie Cockerill, Maud Heel, Nellie Payne, Lily Cockerill, Minnie Ratledge, Rose Kingstone, George Dixon (boy standing)
Front row	Teddy Cockerill, Unity Cockerill, Maggie Green, Edith Heel, Geoffrey Payne, Harry Hillyer, Jessie Timson, seated George Dixon, Headmaster

The school grows too large

The school was expected to cater for 140 children when it was built in 1846. However, George Butler was before his time in wanting to educate all the children. Poverty meant that parents preferred the children to bring in money as soon as they could get a job. With time the concept of education was accepted and although there were rarely over 120 children the school was badly over crowded. More space was required. In 1864 Mr Charles Pilgrim MP of Gayton House donated more land for an enlarged playground on the boys side and the problem was mitigated by the School Master moving out of the school's living accommodation into the White House. The school room was acknowledged as too small for the 100 children who regularly attended plus the 20 infants using the School Master's accommodation. The architect E F Law was employed in the 1870s to enlarge the school building.

A school for infants, boys and girls was built in 1901 and dedicated to Captain Cecil Eykyn (left) who served in the Black Watch and died in the Boer War

School children in 1907

From left to right:

Back row	Violet Hannells, Mrs Linda Kingston's mother, boy, boy, Geoffrey Chester, boy, boy, boy
Second row	Lucy Timson (with bow), Mrs Rogers, Mrs Ethel Folwell, Anne Roberts, Dolly, girl, girl, Mrs Bessie Johnson (standing)
Third row	Emily Newcomb, girl, Connie Chester, girl, girl, girl, Beatrice Inns (seated)
Front row	Five boys

Miss Lucy Timson, school teacher

Lucy Timson (born 8 January 1889 - died 28 October 1979) lived in the Canal House at Banbury Lane with her family and went to Gayton School. In 1903 she was appointed a Monitor, which meant that she learnt her school work and then taught it to the younger children. It was usual to have one Monitor to ten pupils. In 1904 Lucy was accepted as a Pupil Teacher and trained at Northampton High School whilst teaching part-time at Gayton. In June 1907 she passed her Preliminary Certificate. On 2 December 1907 she was appointed Assistant in the Infant School at Milton.

Gayton School between the wars

Hilda and Edie, sisters who attended the school, reckon that school days are the best days of your life. On the face of it this is difficult to understand. Children were given the cane when they had been naughty or, as Hilda had suffered once, a ruler across the knuckles, or 100 lines to write without making any blotches, using a pen with a nib and ink from a well. That was a demanding task. There were no toys to play with at school. From first thing in the morning to last thing in the afternoon 75 years ago, all the children were allowed to do was work! And it all had to be done in the complete silence that Miss Hare insisted upon.

Boy, girl, boy, girl!

In the classroom the 50 or so children sat arranged in cramped rows, boy, girl, boy, girl; an arrangement which left the girls' ankles bruised from encounters with the boys' sturdy boots. In the playground, however, with no teacher on duty as there is today, a high wall prudently separated the boys from the girls and infants. If the door in the middle of the wall was ever unlocked, Hilda and Edie do not remember it!

The Gayton Trust

The painting of the *Laughing Cavalier* by Frans Hals graced the walls of the school room and open fires burned in the grate. Edie recalls being allowed to sit close to the fire one day when she was sent to school with earache. You had to be pretty poorly not to go to school, especially when the reward for good attendance was 6s 8d (33p) paid into your bank book at the end of the year. This was a lot of money in those days. The Gayton Trust (a church charity) also provided £5 to each Gayton child when they left school although this was reduced to £2 in later years. Nonetheless, it helped some girls to buy their aprons and caps when they went to work in service and others used it to train as hairdressers.

The community worked together

In 1936 the Alms Charity paid for Gayton school to have a wireless receiver. It was granted so that the scholars could listen to the new educational programmes. Two years later it was decided to install a new hot water system. The cost was to be £79. There was no National Health Service and families could not always afford the care children needed. Ada Shipperley required a pair of surgical boots and the community raised the money, £1 10s 6d, appropriately with a children's entertainment, and the sum was topped up from the collection in church.

Walking to school

Many youngsters had to walk long distances to and from school. Children came from Banbury Lane, Tiffield and the canal. Only the Cockayne family, coming from O'ful, lived too far away to walk home for lunch and carried with them their bread and jam or syrup to eat. Fortunately for them Phil Kirton's bus which took workers in to Northampton for work in the morning was returning to Eastcote at a suitable time to take them up the Milton Road hill. But they still had a long walk home, albeit downhill.

So, why did Hilda and Edie enjoy school so much?

Hilda and Edie's teacher was kind and fair and school work was much better than all the chores they had to do at home for their parents. For example, each evening after school they had to help their mother with the housework, fetch water and do some cooking and, when it was dark, early to bed. They did have time to play with toys on the way to and from school. A hoop could be rolled along with a stick, and marbles, hopscotch and skipping ropes were popular. The really talented children could whip a top and keep it spinning all the way from the school to Park Lane but of course, there were no cars to worry about.

Gayton School 1935

From left to right:

Back row   Bill Jacobs, Stan Roberts, Cyril Hillyer, Ron Webb, Peter Butcher, Brian Cokayne

Second row   Kath Smith, Roger East, Clarence Roberts, Joan Smith, Ena Davis, Gladys White, Dinah Marston, Jean Smith, Olive Folwell, David Roberts, Jack Paul

Third row   Joan Sturgess, Betty Sturgess, Betty Marston, Violet Munton, Mary Roberts, Marjorie Smith, Barbara Moore, Margaret Puxley, Lavinia Moore, Audrey Folwell, Enid White, Jean Goosey, Pauline Wills

Front row   Ray Cockerill, John Marston, Bill Munton, Walt Newcomb, Brian Ratledge, Eric Cockerill, Richard Marston, Ken Cokayne, Maurice Billing, John Wright, Eric White, Ray Newcomb, Ron Goosey

Evacuees brought illnesses from the towns

In a small rural population children were not exposed to as many serious illnesses as town children. But with the arrival in 1940-41 of urban evacuees, Gayton suffered a measles epidemic. In February 1941, the death of Grace Judith Mansfield aged two years was attributed to diphtheria. Only the day before it appeared that she had nothing more than a bad cold. As it had been eight years since any child had died in Gayton it was keenly felt. The authorities were worried about a national diphtheria epidemic and the children were inoculated in February and March. In July there was an outbreak of Whooping Cough.

Threatened with closure

The shortcomings of rural education were exposed during the Second World War. The city dwellers were horrified at the antiquated facilities, and the authorities disappointed by the quality of education. In 1947 the County Education Committee issued their development plan. Gayton School was to be closed but not until 1959-67. The seniors would be going to Roade and the juniors and infants to Blisworth. In 1951 the School Managers applied for Aided Status to keep the school open as long as possible. In 1952 it was granted controlled status. Gayton School fought to keep open and survived.

School children seated around Miss Bamford and her dog, Trixie, in 1947

From left to right:
Back row   Mervyn Cockerill, Peter Fisher, Beryl Keenes, Maureen Barker, Terry Webb, Barry Hillyard
Middle row   Malcolm Cockayne, Peter Battams, Daphne Hillyard, Kate Carney, Miss Bamford, Ruth Cockerill, Marina Wills, Bobby Paul, girl
Front row   Gillian Donnay, Elizabeth Stanley, Jennifer Nightingale, Jane Kingston, Christine Cockerill, Ann Munton, Pat Payne, Yvonne Donnay

Ups and downs of school life

In 1982 concerns arose between the head teacher and some of the parents about swimming for the children, and dogs fouling the school grounds. Everything was eventually resolved. A new head teacher came to the school but many of the children had been removed to Blisworth school and for some years the number of children attending Gayton school was very low. Since then the school's reputation has climbed and quite the reverse occurs with children being driven to Gayton from Hunsbury to share the very high standard of village education.

Schoolchildren with the Maypole when there were outhouses in the playground

School children 1969

From left to right:
Back row   David Wilkins, Andrew Fowler, Richard Berridge, Peter Payne, Lesley Munns, Susan Shepherd, Mark
              Goatley, Ian Fraser, Philip Ratledge, Nicholas Allen
Middle row   Pamela Gould, Rachel East, Sandra Goodyer, Shani Fowler, Pauline Ratledge, Susan Woolston,
              Katherine East, Jackie Gould, Debbie Read, Dawn Fraser
Front row   Martin Saxilby, Peter Saxilby, Mark Briglin, David Ratledge, Graham Taylor, Philip East, Stuart
              Woolston

School children 1969

From left to right:
- Back row   Karl Hillyard, Toby Berridge, Theo East, Martyn Gould, David Goodyer, Mark Ratledge, Claire Newcomb, Wendy Simmons, Nicola Fowler
- Middle row   Joanne Woolston, Vivienne Cross, Lesley Gould, Donna Hall, Mary Knight, Susan Cross, Gary Reid
- Front row   Kathleen Ratledge, Adrian Briglin, David Parish, Gillian Woolston, Joanne Fowler, Colin Reid

Classroom concentration in 1969

School children 1984

From left to right:
Back row   Mrs Goatley, Martin Poxon, Neil Bailey, Paul Clarke, James Foster, Chris Baldham, Martin Wilcox, Mark Holland, Gareth Poxon, Miss Lane

Front row   Liam Hollin, Alice Fox, Benedict Hayes, Sonia A'court, Carl McDonald, Stephen A'court, Andrew Cohen, Rebecca Fox

Learning through role play in 1984

Gayton School 1991

From left to right:

Back row	Mrs Julie Osborne, Mrs Helen Bestwick, Jason Carter, Stephen Bayliss, Dan Jeffery, Matthew Crouch, Matthew Carter, Katie Foster, Sarah Mallock, Melissa Hunt, Paula Barnett, Karen Rowe, Mrs Pam North
Second row	Patrick Hoy, Simon Barnett, Gemma Clinch, Anna Foster, Sarah James, Peter Gould, Natalie Hayman, Christopher Platt, Stephen Gould, Paul Quinn
Third row	Gemma Morrell, James Price, Emma Robinson, Tod Jeffery, Simon Hunt, Adam Barnett, Andrew Crouch, Somerset Hoy, Hannah Almond, Scott Riley, Amy Richards
Front row	Helen Robinson, Owain Richards, Luke Jeffery, Jennifer East, Michael Quinn, Dawn Morrell

Learning through practical experience in 1991

Technology in the 1927 schoolroom

Technology in the 1999 schoolroom

A Village of Farms

The early farms

Two great fields, East and West

Life in medieval times revolved around getting enough to eat. Consequently farming was at the centre of village life. Before 1313 two great fields in Gayton were cultivated, East and West field. Whilst one grew crops, the other was left fallow.

Catwel Feld, Drynel Feld and Milne Feld

By 1388 a three field system had been introduced. Change was brought about because of the need to produce more food, rather than to compensate for the loss of farm workers in the Black Death. The manor's farm land was dispersed amongst all three fields.

Enclosure in the 1600s

Enclosure, the dividing up of Gayton's large communal farming areas into smaller separate fields, took place extremely early. It was noted in the Parish Register that:

> ...the 23rd day of March Anoo dmii 1600 of Elizabeth Regina 43 it was agreed and concluded upon by the whole consort as well as Mr Francis Tanfield as by the rest of the freeholders and townsmen of the parishe of Gayton that upon the agreement of the inclosing of the feilds of Gayton into severall plotts there was a severall plott set out and measured to the quantitie of ten acres or thereabouts in lewe of as much as before lay in divers places of the saide fields always accounted and used as towne grounds before time to the behoof and proffitt of the said towne of Gayton...

This was witnessed by John Tanfielde, John Markes Rector of Gayton, John Marriot, John Pacie, Edward Houghton churchwarden, John Markes, John Watson, and Thomas Stones. The individual holdings were 'now enclosed, fenced, and ditched with mounds'.

Money to be made

In the 1600s new methods were being put forward to improve quality and yield. It was not practical for landowners to try out these ideas in large open fields where everyone farmed jointly. Where stock ran together, controlled breeding could not take place and all the animals were at risk from the diseased and sickly.

The rich benefited but did the poor suffer?

Enclosure benefited the affluent in the village, but not the poor. What is unclear is whether the poor really suffered from Enclosure. Also, did the rent from the ten acres of land known as the Town Ground, which was put aside for their benefit, compensate them? The Alms Ground Account Book recorded by name the amount given to the poorest in the village from the Town Ground rent money. But we do not know if this made up for everyone's lost rights.

Who signed for enclosure and why?

Francis Tanfield was lord of the manor in 1600. (See page 6) His heir, William Tanfield, sold the manor of Gayton to Sir William and Richard Samwell soon after enclosure. In 1606, William would have received a much better price for the manor because the land was already enclosed.

John Markes was the Rector (and a rich Gentleman)

The Markes family were well-to-do yeoman farmers. Theodore and James, John Markes' sons, were running a dairy farming business in 1609. If they were hoping to improve their stock they would have been keen for the fields to be enclosed. It enabled them to keep their herd separate from weak cattle owned by the poorer members of the community.

John Watson

The Watson family also had an interest in quality cattle as William and Jane Watson were supplying their own butcher's shop. It flourished so that when he died, in 1711, William left his 'cows, bullocks and shops and house' equally shared between his many grandchildren.

Thomas Stones

The Stones family of Silston owned land in Gayton.

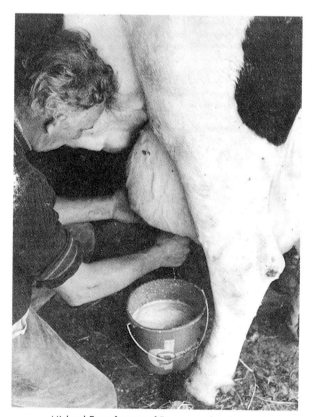

Michael East, farmer of Evergreen, hard at work

John Pacie and Edward Houghton

Edward Houghton's relations were extensive landowners. Many pieces of land carried their name such as Houghton Barn Close, and 'land I bought from John Houghton the Elder'. Even the new lord of the manor, Richard Samwell, purchased 24 acres from John Houghton before 1661. The two families united when John Houghton married Margaret Pacie on 26 August 1626. Margaret Houghton inherited the Squirrel Inn in 1701 and needed the custom of the yeoman farmers.

John Marriot

The Marriot family owned land and passed a farm in Gayton down through the generations until the end of the nineteenth century. They held office in the parish. In 1675 a John Marriot was Parish Constable (see presentment below) and in 1686 he died leaving his residence, Conduit House, to his family.

Presentment of 1675 when the Parish Canstable was John Marriot

1   The Constable there Presents Patience Pell for beinge an Inmate.
2   That ye highwayes and Bridges there are in good repaire.
3   That watch and ward there and hue and Crys have bin duely observed.
4   That no Ryots, Routs or Unlawfull assemblys have bin Comitted there.
5   That there are no Popish recusants there.
        Patience Pell presented as above.

Wealth creation

The early enclosure seems to have achieved everything the farmers would have wished and there is evidence that they became significantly richer. Ultimately it was the farmhouses in the village that benefited. Throughout the 1700s new larger farmhouses were built such as Thomas Marriot's house now called Fiveways. Others were enlarged and restored like Evergreen until, as with Home Farm, it is difficult to tell whether it has been extended or rebuilt! Whatever the case, all the old materials would have been recycled.

The Paynes and the Georges

The name of Payne has been linked with the village from as early as 1591 when John Payne was Robert Tanfield's tenant-at-will. The Paynes and the Georges were from the seventeenth century a major force in Gayton's farming community. By intermarrying with enthusiasm and moving between the farms frequently, in many cases it is difficult to distinguish between the two.

Fiveways and Outback

A story of two houses

Thomas Marriot was living in the house now called Outback, on Back Lane, at the time of his death in 1785. Next door was his 'farmhouse', now called Fiveways. He left both buildings, the 'adjoining yards, stables, outhouses, orchards, gardens, barns, rickyards and buildings' to his wife during her life and then to his granddaughter, Ann Griffith. Ann's husband, William, continued Thomas Marriot's farming.

Pheasant Griffith inherited Fiveways

Ann and William's son, Pheasant, was left the 'dwelling house with the yard, garden, orchard' (Fiveways) which was being rented by Revd Elderton. But the house in which William Griffith had lived (Outback) had been sold to Matthew Charles. However, he rented it back to Pheasant Griffith who continued running his father's farm. In 1851 that farm consisted of 110 acres of land concentrated mainly near the Banbury Lane. Pheasant Griffith died in 1878.

Ivy House

Mrs Roberts

Edmund Roberts was a building contractor and farmer. By 1885 he had bought Fiveways which he renamed Ivy House. The architect Thomas Tew added the Flemish gable which was copied from his work at Stoke Park. With his son in 1891, Roberts' company restored the church porch. After his wife's death, Edmund Roberts married Mrs Lovell, a widow. As Mrs Roberts she outlived her husband and became notorious when, aged 97, she was still able to crack nuts, with her teeth. Mr A J Bennett of the Royal Insurance Company bought Ivy House c1915 and over the next 40 years the house saw a greater turnover of occupiers than any other village property. In the 1950s Mr Garnham divided the house into two and each half was sold separately.

Outback and Fiveways in the foreground c1900. Outback (formerly called Laurel Cottage) was the original farmhouse but when the farm prospered a newer bigger building was constructed. Later, Thomas Tew added ornamental gables.

Manor or farmhouse?

It was not until 1751 when Samwell sold the manor to Richard Kent that the manor-house was first rented out. Eight years later William Payne was living in the manor-house farming 201 acres of Dr Hawley's land. William Payne died before 1764 and his widow, Elizabeth, married William George of Home Farm. This marriage united the two largest farms in Gayton. However, both spouses had children from their previous relationships and the farms did not merge into one but remained separate. Each was farmed by the sons of the family. Elizabeth's son, William Payne, married Charlotte and continue to run the manor farm. When William died, Charlotte with her younger sons, John, James and Thomas continued farming the 260 acre Manor Farm which employed three men and three boys. Responsibility was passed down from brother to brother until 1884 when Thomas finally retired and moved out of the manor-house into East View.

The manor as a private house

As a private house once more the manor had a quick turn over of tenants. Robert McClure was succeeded by William Thomas Fawcus Hill and his wife Kate. A few years later, in 1893, when Revd Arthur Butler visited the village Miss Bickmore had made it her home, and according to Butler had made the rooms look 'really lovely' and 'all for £40 a year'. But whether that was Miss Bickmore's income or the rent of the property is not clear. The gates were reported 'poor' in 1910, although the drains were in good working order and for a time Joseph Major-Lucas and his cousin, Mrs Meredith lived there.

The Manor house c1920

The George family

Mr and Mrs Jack George re-introduced the farming connection but their lifestyle was not that of the farmhouse. With the last of the Paynes retiring, for a few years the George's held sway, but their activities centred on Home Farm where Bill George lived. The era ended with a big sale of George family stock in 1924, when over 500 lots of household furniture, modern and antique, were auctioned. The house became the home of its owner and occupied by Mrs Hawley and her two sons, Sir David and Anthony. The major farmer both of the Manor farm and Home Farm became Frank Chester. When Sir David returned in 1946, after being a prisoner of war, the Hawleys left the village. The manor was once again let, this time, to Mr Leslie Church and his wife.

Evergreen Farm

The George and Payne families

It is possible that Thomas George took over Evergreen Farm from his father, Samuel, when he died in 1803 and farmed for 43 years until his own death in 1846. William Payne junior moved to Evergreen Farm in 1847. He was the eldest son of William and Charlotte Payne of Manor Farm. William senior died soon afterwards and Charlotte and the younger boys continued farming the Manor. William, with his wife Ann, farmed 140 acres at Evergreen employing four labourers. The farm grew to 165 acres employing two men and three boys until Ann, now widowed, was unable to continue.

A 'nice house'

George and Harriet Dunckley had been living at Evergreen Farm for over a decade when, in 1893, Arthur Butler visited Gayton. George Dunckley senior was a retired builder and Butler's comments that Dunckley was slowly recovering the use of his foot, may shed some light on the cause for Dunckley's retirement. Butler also commented on the 'nice house' they lived in. Their son, George, was the farmer and also a prominent Freemason. Four men worked for George junior on the farm, Webb, Hillyer, Ratledge and Dunckley and they drew the bier which carried his coffin when he died from heart disease, aged 55, in 1912.

Evergreen Farm c1908 with the Red Lion in the background

Five up, three down

In 1914 Evergreen Farm was described as, 'Houses, two attics, five rooms up, three rooms down, kitchen, scullery, dairy, gig house, harness room, cow shed, cart stable, chaff barn, open hovel and cart hovel'. The buildings that form today's Evergreen Stables, across the road from the farm, are included in this inventory as the outhouses surrounding the dairy.

Henry Ernest Christian East

Henry East's family were brewers in Milton and he moved from running the Royal Oak, Blisworth to Evergreen Farm. By 1936 he had retired to Outback and handed over his enterprises to his two sons, Ernest Christian East, who farmed Evergreen Farm, and Herbert William East, Hillcrest Farm. Today Evergreen Farm is farmed by Ernie East's son, Michael.

Henry East working on the farm

Home Farm

In 1759 William George (1721-78) was farming 215 acres of Dr Hawley's land. After his wife died, he married Elizabeth Payne bringing together, in 1764, two farming families. His son, also William, farmed briefly and married in Gayton before moving to Edgeware where he stabled the Northampton coach. He may even have driven it sometimes! By 1820 Home Farm was being run by his sons, William and Joseph George, before being passed down to William's son, Walter.

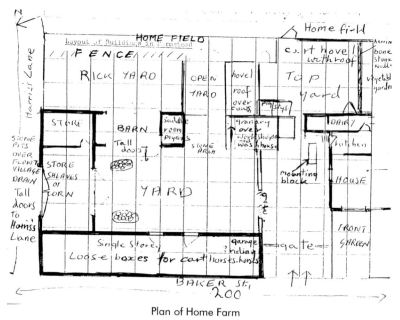

Plan of Home Farm

Walter George (1814-75)

Walter George had taken over the running of Home Farm by 1841. His Account Book details his trade with other villagers. For example, he sold a five year old chestnut horse that he had bred himself to Colin Fitzroy for £75. In 1856 he bought his coal from Mr Chamberlain at Banbury Lane. He paid Saul Saull, the cooper from Corner Cottage, for churns. He employed Elizabeth Storey the Gayton nursemaid, and paid George Inns for drilling 15 acres of wheat.

Prize winning horses, sheep and pigs

Walter George handed Home Farm down to his sons, also called William and Joseph! William was particularly interested in breeding horses and sheep. Two of his horses graced the King's stables and he had the distinction of having won the first race at the opening of the Towcester Steeplechase with Ploughboy on which his brother Joe was jockey. Joseph embarked on a journey to Africa on 4 December 1873 but his father seeing him off at Liverpool docks, stopped him from going due to the last minute news that 19 of the 20 ex-patriots there had died of fever. Walter wrote that he could not let him go.

Home Farm

Bill George with his groom, Henry 'Bozzy' Cowley outside
the stables at Home Farm

The farmyard was dismantled when the farm was sold as a
private house in September 1977

Alderman William George (1849-1916)

William George had a famous flock of Oxford Downs and for 30 years took many awards, and on three occasions won the champion prize for best tenant farmer's sheep at the Northampton Fat Stock Show. His black Berkshire pigs won cups as well. A staunch Conservative, he was Chairman of the Parish Council, Vice-Chairman of the Rural District Council and from May 1907 Alderman of the County Council. Alderman William George died in 1916.

Bill and Jack George

The farm passed to William's sons Jack and Bill. Jack George moved into the manor in about 1917 whilst his brother Bill lived at Home Farm. The Georges farmed approximately 600 acres. In 1924 they sold the farms and Jack moved from the manor into a new house he had built, Great Grounds, Milton Road. He went on to build Tudor Cottage, Back Lane where he and his wife lived for a short time before moving to London and separating.

Harris' Lane

William Harris rented houses and lanes from Henry Hawley in 1759, He did not, however, rent any land.

In 1759 William Harris rented a lane as well as a house from Henry Hawley.
This footpath is called locally Harris' Lane.

Old Manor Farm

By 1841 another William Harris was the owner and occupier of what is called today Old Manor Farm, High Street. One of the outhouses, that has been used more recently as a butcher's shop, has a date stone of 1734. The farm grew to 63 acres in 1851. William Harris' health deteriorated with age and John Cole took over the small holding. By the end of the century the house had fallen into disrepair and was divided into two cottages one of which housed Mary Dunckley, the school needlework teacher, and the other, George Kingston, the carrier.

Pigs killed in the pub yard

Frank Chester ran a public house in Blisworth before he moved to Gayton in about 1898 to run the Crown and Squirrel. It seems strange today that the pub yard was used for his butcher's business. Harry George's father worked for the Chesters slaughtering animals in the pub yard for some years.

Frank Chester, on the right, with his butcher's cart outside the family business

A butcher's shop

In 1906 Frank Chester moved his butcher's business to Old Manor Farm. He turned one of the buildings into a butcher's shop and knocked the cottages back into one farmhouse. Here too, animals were butchered in the yard. Tales of the awful squeals of the pigs being killed are still remembered today. Frank Chester's horse and cart was the equivalent of the modern mobile shops that visit the villages. Frank and his sons travelled around selling meat in all the surrounding villages.

The Chester family
Left to right:
Back row Jack, Lyndsay and Aubrey, the three sons
Front row Frank, daughter Connie, and Alice

F A Chester and sons, farmer

Home Farm had been empty for some time when in 1935 Frank's son, Aubrey Chester, moved there when he married Miss Higgerson, the school mistress. Manor Farm was taken over and the Chester family took over from the George's as the main farmers in the village.

Rensbury

Two views of Rensbury

William Rolfe

It is likely that William Rolfe moved to Gayton at the turn of the nineteenth century. He was a farmer and baker who bought his own house and land, although he rented additional farm land on the Eastcote parish boundary in 1841. When his son, Richard, took over the farming, Edmund Kirby Linnell became baker.

Farm fire at Flitnells

A fire can be a financial blow to a farmer. In November 1863 Richard Rolfe had a fire at his field barn at Flitnells. It also destroyed several outhouses, a rick of wheat the produce of five acres, a stuck of oats the produce of five acres and a stuck of 'Alsack' seed (this may have been 'alsike', a red clover) and bean straw. The fire was made worse by it being 'a dreadful windy night'. Richard's father William R Rolfe, told Walter George that he suspected arson. The insurance paid £140.

Other farm fires in Gayton

During the First World War when Gayton Scouts were guarding the railway bridges they spotted a rick fire at Wood Farm. Lives and property were undoubtedly saved when they ran promptly for assistance. The Gammage Brothers farming Wood Farm at this time were far from popular and this could easily have been arson, too. More recently in October 1972 a series of five barns, full of hay and straw, were set on fire. The fourth barn to be set alight was at Hillcrest Farm. A Dutch barn containing 250 tons of hay and 5,000 bales of straw was destroyed along with four hen-houses and farm equipment.

Glebe Farm

A farm house was built by the church on land that provided the rector with his living when a mortgage was taken out on 29 May 1877. Another on 26 September 1882 enabled a barn to be converted into a cottage on the farm. In about 1888 John Kingston, a butcher and farmer, rented the farm from the Revd King. He used the farmhouse as a butcher's shop.

Glebe Farm

Suicide at Glebe Farm

After farming for 25 years, John Kingston at 69 years old caused a sensation in the village by committing suicide c1914. It was said that he was deeply depressed following his wife's death, three months earlier. He placed the barrel of a shot gun in his mouth and pulled the trigger. The grizzly episode was reported in great detail. 'Mr Kingston's skull was completely blown off, and blood and brains were scattered on the four walls of the room.' John Kingston's household furniture, agricultural implements and farm stock was sold by auction and the demand for his horses was such that a black mare of six years raised 33 guineas.

Hillcrest Farm's barn and its contents burnt down

Hillcrest Farm

George Moore took over farming the Glebe Farm. Henry East bought the farm from the Church c1917, re-named it Hillcrest Farm and his sons Roger and Herbert farmed it. Another house called Windy Ridge was built on the farm between the World Wars.

Gayton Wood Farm

George Travill, a tenant of Dr Hawley, farmed Gayton Wood Farm using one barn as a weaver's shop. His businesses may have been a success but his family life was not. In 1759 he married Ann Parker. As his wife, she would be entitled to a portion of her husband's estate if he died. However his son Richard and new wife, Ann, did not get on. Richard, wishing to exclude Ann from her inheritance, managed to extract a letter from his father disallowing Ann her one third share of the estate. By March 1776 George was a sick man and whatever Ann's faults she redeemed herself by caring for her husband in his illness. George was torn between wife and son. In his will he emphasised how much he loved Ann and how devotedly she had nursed him through his sickness. He reinstated her right to a third of his estate.

Richard Travill

Ironically Richard Travill died a few months later. He left his goods first to his wife, Elisabeth, née Gudgeon of Blisworth, whom he had married in 1763, for her lifetime and then to her sister, Ann's children. It is evident that Richard and Elisabeth had no surviving children as Richard distributed his estate widely.

Thomas West farmed Travill land

Thomas West took over from his uncle, Richard, and was renting the 157 acres of Hawley land that Travill had farmed by 1801. His two sons, Thomas and William took over, inheriting, in addition, John Wheatley's property in 1817, through their mother, Ann, who was John Wheatley's sister.

From farming to ironstone mining and back!

Gayton Wood Farm continued to be farmed by the West family until all the land was taken over for ironstone mining. The farmhouse became a farm labourer's cottage and housed a shepherd until the Bailiff for the ironstone works, James Hillyard, moved in.

The Gammage Brothers

In 1903 the Gammage brothers began farming the land again and gradually as the ironstone mining declined the farm was built up. Jack and Perridge Gammage were a violent unpleasant pair. They were not good employers and maltreated their young workers, the two Cox brothers and William Harris. During the first World War they had two prisoners of war as well as four civilians working on the land. Towcester racecourse had recently opened and they owned several thoroughbred steeplechasers. The George's took over the farm and today it is the home of Mr and Mrs Huckerby.

Medieval fishpond at Gayton Wood Farm in January 1992

Old Wilds or New Wilds?

In 1630 Robert Tanfield sold a group of fields to Matthias Wheelowes. George Blonde was farming this land but was succeeded by John Frost. Then Bernard Francklin became the tenant and married Hannah Bayley from a family of Gayton yeoman farmers, in September 1721. We do not know whether he was at Old Wilds, New Wilds or even Woods Farm.

John Wheatley at New Wilds
When in 1782 Thomas Wheatley left his son, John, his farming equipment they may have been farming Gayton Wilds Farm together. A year later John was sufficiently well off to marry. Mary Wheatley, née Atkinson, died soon afterwards, perhaps in childbirth, and in 1785 John married Abigail Maddock. Through Abigail, in 1801, John inherited a share in Samuel Maddock's estate. Although Samuel Maddock farmed he lived in the centre of the village in a house that later became the Red Lion.

Thomas West at Wood Farm and William West at Wilds Farm
William West took over from John Wheatley at Gayton Wilds whilst his brother Thomas West continued with Gayton Wood Farm, the family farm. William married Harriott and their son William continued with the farm.

Kenning's farm
When William West junior died his daughter's husband Harry Kenning ran the farm. The land, as elsewhere in Gayton, was gradually turned over to ironstone mining but the daughters, 'The Miss Kennings' as they were known locally, continued to live at the farmhouse until well into the 1950s. The land had gradually been returned to farming and the farmhouse was taken over by Ken East and now continues in his son Ricky's hands.

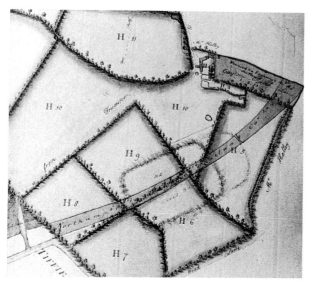

John Darker's Estate map of 1791.
John Wheatley rented land and Wilds Farm.

Cutting the sheaves of corn using a Nuffield tractor with a
Perkins engine and pulling a binder

Gayton Wilds farmhouse in 1994

Old Wilds

Elizabeth George rented the Old Wilds in 1791 with some farm land. At this time it was only a small dwelling compared to the Wilds, where John Wheatley lived, and which was described as a homestead. Old Wilds became a farmworker's cottage for Gammages' farm (Gayton Wood Farm). It had no services and all water had to be carried from the village.

Old Wilds in December 1993

The Weir

The Weir is in the centre of the village, at Fiveways. It was named after an ancient pond that used to be opposite on the other side of High Street. On the map, it looks like a traditional village pond. Today the area close to that spot is very prone to flooding.

James Payne

James Payne's older brother William farmed the Manor Farm with his wife Charlotte whilst James and his wife, Alice, farmed at the Weir. Today, it is difficult to imagine the Weir as a farmhouse surrounded by farm buildings. The garden wall on the Baker Street side was once the back of a row of cottages. They enclosed the cobbled farmyard now under the side lawn. There were other outhouses but one barn still survives having been converted into a house called Instone, Baker Street. In 1851 the farm was 167 acres and employed six labourers. Living with James junior was his sister Mary. His cousin William farmed Evergreen, his cousin Thomas farmed the Manor, and his brother Thomas ran the Red Lion just around the corner.

At one time the Weir was a farmhouse with its farmyard to the right of this photograph. Today, what appears to be a porch in the centre of the house is a buttress to support the bulging wall.

Change of fortune

Between 1851 and 1891 it is not clear who lived at the Weir. It is possible the farm started falling into disrepair when James Payne retired. There is also a possibility that George Dunckley lived there. He may even have farmed there for a while although he would have been quite an old man at the time. In approximately 1891 the house was sold to Mr Roberts of Ivy House (Fiveways) who also owned Outback. He rented the Weir to Emanuel Ratledge. Some time after 1912 William Ratledge, with his wife Elizabeth, pictured above, moved in.

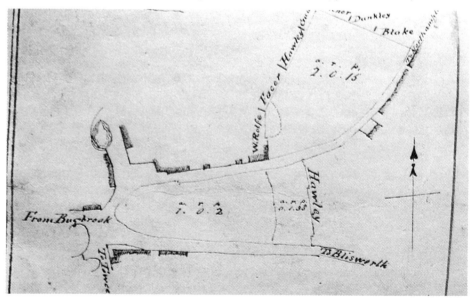

An early nineteenth-century deed shows the oval pond at Fiveways from which the Weir takes its name

Instone

Instone was converted from a barn in 1923 by William Ratledge

Retirement home

William Ratledge converted this former barn, in 1923, into a home for his sister-in-law, Annie Ratledge wife of John Ratledge, baker. She had been appointed Head Teacher on 1 May 1902. Accommodation was provided for her when School House was built in 1909 with an endowment left by Mrs Kennard in the 1840s. The building of the house was precipitated by the risk of the endowment being taken into county funds by the School Board. When Annie Ratledge retired after 26 years as a respected Head Mistress she needed her own home. William Ratledge was a builder and able to have the work done.

Goggs Farm

Farmyard and barn

In 1841 Pheasant Griffiths was farming the land around Goggs Farm. This land was owned by Matthew Charles. Griffiths died in 1878 and a farm bailiff called Isaac Lovell moved into The Goggs. By 1891 the farm had been bought by Henry Lucas, and his three sons Charles, John and Frederick helped him on the farm.

Two brothers marry two sisters

Living in the village was George Old a shoemaker who made boots for the bargemen for legging the Blisworth canal tunnel. He was well known locally as a preacher who walked out to the villages, preaching for the last time in Evenden before his death on 9 September

1893. He and his wife, Ann, had two daughters Jane and Emily who married the two brothers Charles and Frederick Lucas. Frederick Lucas followed in his father-in-law's footsteps as a Methodist preacher, often taking the service at Gayton's Chapel. His daughter, Gladys, became school teacher and then postmistress.

The Parish family

Charles Lucas took over the farm from his father. The house was described c1914 as having '4 rooms upstairs and 3 downstairs'. Outside was a variety of outhouses comprising two barns, a stable, a cart shed, and two open hovels. The livestock kept were pigs, cows and calves. By 1936 Charles Lucas had retired from farming and Frank and Thomas Parish had bought the farm. Frank's sons Reg and Charles took over the farming until finally Charles retired in September 1994.

Wendy Briglin visiting Goggs Farm in 1994

Farming and the Second World War

Low wages, high costs

Between the two world wars, agricultural wages in England fell not only in relation to other workers but below the poverty line. However, the cost of wages to the farmer was high and inevitably jobs disappeared.

More food was part of the war effort

The onset of the Second World War was to change all that. Gone was the Government's laissez-faire attitude, the country needed food and the farmers had to provide it. Demands were made of farmers which under normal conditions would have been unthinkable. More land had to be turned over to producing crops which Gayton managed to do.

Gayton produces more
Being a mixed farming area the number of cattle was relatively low but Gayton's farmers illustrated their improved efficiency by managing, in addition to a greater variety and acreage of crops, a very gradual increase in cattle numbers, as well, during the war years.

Women's work
Women in the villages were encouraged to help in the fields. In July 1940, Mrs Hawley gave a talk to the WI on the 'Land Army' and urged the women to use any spare time to help the farmers in the fields. The Women's Land Army was gradually accepted by the farmers and drafted in.

Child labour
When necessary children were given holidays from school to help and the *Mercury and Herald* reported that in Northamptonshire thousands of children, many of them evacuees, had been gathering acorns, horse-chestnuts and beech mast to feed Britain's pigs.

More tractors, less horses
The nation's farmers mechanised farming in an attempt to ease the shortage of agricultural workers. The four tractors that could be seen working the land in 1940 in Gayton increased in the following year to five. This trend to mechanisation was to continue, as the drop in production of oats after 1941 probably indicates and Britain became 'the most highly mechanised farming country in the world'.

Frank Wakelin and Harry Rook grass mowing with a new 1942 model Fordson tractor and trailed grass mower

Binding sheaves

Hay carts have many uses

Steam threshing

Charles Shipperley, from Brittains Cottages, ploughing with a one furrow plough

Left to right: Ernie Garrett, Cyril Smith and Bob Mansfield on Ernie East's farm. The cereal crop had been cut, stood up, in what is locally called 'shocks', and left for a fortnight before being brought, by drays, into the rickyard ready to be built into ricks.

A group of Chester's farm workers

Left to right:
Back row   George Wickham, Ted Cockerill, Joan Woods (Smith)
            Bill West, May Carney
Front row   Evelyn Cockerill, and Gladys White (Green)

Evelyn Cockerill piling mangolds outside Manor Farm. The mangolds were put through a shredder and mixed with 'chaff' to be fed to 'cows and beasts'.

Left to right: Tony Rogers and dog Sally, Ken Cokayne, Blossom the horse, Bill West and Trevor Cokayne at Eight Acres, The Wilds, c1946

Land Army girl, Phyllis Rose Dale, who married Ken Cokayne c1944

Ted Paul tossing hay onto a baler. A group of land army girls from the Kislingbury Hostel were helping on Herbert East's farm.

Ernie Garrett, George Dixon and Charlie Rook at Evergreen farm

Eat more potatoes

The Ministry of Food attached great importance to the potato crop, but they required not only the farmers to change their ways, but the public had to be persuaded to eat the potatoes produced. The better drained light red soil at the top of Gayton Hill was suitable for the crop and substantial quantities of potatoes were planted during the war years. It was, however, very seasonal and everybody was required to help at potato planting and picking times.

Potato picking

The older primary school children, including evacuees, were officially allowed time off from school at the request of the farmer to the Secretary for Education (as per Circular 1385 LEA) and with permission from parents. Gayton's increased potato production meant that the school was closed for a 'potato lifting holiday'. As local potatoes became available advertisements were placed by the Ministry of Food in the local newspapers to increase consumption by reminding the public constantly that 'Every time you eat potatoes instead of bread you release food ships for vital war work'.

The pretty little fields disappeared

Agriculture had changed dramatically during the war years with the farmers now efficiently producing a wider variety of crops whilst still maintaining their stock, but how did this affect the appearance of the countryside? Hilda Billing remembers the fields of pre-war Gayton as 'pretty little fields with lots of cowslips, harebells and bluebells' whilst during the war, her abiding memory is of potato fields, perhaps because of the villagers' involvement with the back breaking job of potato lifting. After the war the fields changed to corn as the potato crop was reduced. However the country's food policy had changed as was demonstrated in 1947 when the Agriculture Act gave farmers the security of assured prices and guaranteed markets, and farmworkers the promise of a living wage and proper housing.

Evergreen stable girls, Emma Ratledge, Kate Cooke and Eleanor Mallock at a sponsored ride event c1995

Working Locally

Brickworks

Banbury Lane Brickworks

The first brickworks in Gayton was established at Banbury Lane. With the need for bricks for the main-line railway bridges it was quite extensive when Eli Smith was brick maker in 1838. However there was soon competition. Sir J H Hawley leased a field by the side of the canal on Corner Piece, for the purpose of brick manufacture, to James Wells of Northampton, coal and corn merchant at £30 *per annum* for 21 years from 6 November 1852. This new business was set up on what is now the site of the old tip on the Milton Road and destined to grow.

Old Brickyard Cottage, Milton Road

The terms of the agreement were that, within six months, Wells would build, 'in a workman like and substantial manner... a dwelling house/cottage at a cost of at least £100'. A cottage was built which survived the years. When the Cokayne family moved out in 1936 it was left empty until the war. Evacuees were moved in temporarily. A Council tip was started to re-fill the pits from which the clay had been removed, and the first manager became the last tenant of the old brickyard house.

Industrial pollution

Walter George farmed Corner Piece, although he called it Calf Close, and by 1853 Mr Wells and Company had turned these fields into a steam brickworks. It was well placed to provide the huge number of bricks required by the Northampton and Banbury Junction Railway. A further agreement with Joseph Adnitt of Northampton, corn merchant and seed crusher, extended the brickworks for 21 years at £75 *per annum* from 28 February 1854. Between 1855 and 1861 Walter George was paid £1 per year compensation by Mr Whitworth of the Brick and Tile Company for the damage done to the pasture. And later he received £4 from Mr Norman for another year. Thomas Collins of Gayton applied for letters patent for the invention of improvements in manufacturing bricks and tiles in 1854.

The Northamptonshire Brick and Tile Company

The brickworks was managed from 1861 by John Pearson who lived at Brick Yard House with his wife, Catherine, and their family. Later Evered J Brown, who became a senior member of the local lodge of the National United Order of Free Gardeners took over and lived at the brickworks with his wife, Emma, two children, Emmerline and Emma, and a local girl, Sarah Loakes, who worked for them. The works, locally called Brown's, consisted of five small rectangular kilns and a large circular Hoffman kiln, 120 foot in diameter. The company had a wharf in Weston Street, Northampton and used its canal-side site in Gayton for transportation. In the later years the fire man was Benjamin Botterill, Harry Wooton was assistant brickmaker, and Samuel Saunders, John Blunt and William Kingston were site labourers.

Decline of the Brick and Tile Company

By 1901 more land was required and Sir H M Hawley leased the field to the west of the brickworks and land for a brickworks in Gayton for 21 years from 8 May 1901 at £80 per *annum* plus royalty, to Evered Brown, brick company manager, and Harry John Butcher, architect. They also leased land on the other side of the road in Buttersley Meadow with permission to use the spring water there. In about 1914 the brickworks was dismantled. It was quite an industrial area by this time. A chimney 200 feet high was demolished by Mr Asplin and all the bricks were re-used in the tramway extension at Far Cotton which was taking place at the time.

Henry Martin Ltd

Between the wars, a new brickworks opened across the road from the tip, and the house now called The Limes was built. In the 1920s the works provided employment for many of the village men. Men like Jack Paul who had to cycle to Piddington to collect his wages, where Henry Martin had a threshing engine and steam roller business.

Martin's brickyard with Lou Bull from Post Office Row driving

The brickmen at Martin's brickyard

Left to right:
Back row   Bill Gostelow, Ernie Dunckley, Bill 'Lap' Webster, Tom Powell
Front row   Jack Paul

Looking down on Martin's brickyard
from the village

Harry 'Nobby' George

Ted and Nancy Paul outside the Dower House where Nancy worked for Mrs Eykyn

Chuff, chuff, chuff!

Wet clay was wire-cut into rows of identical bricks. Men pushed the grid cutter backwards and forwards through the thick chunk of clay cutting in both directions. The wet bricks were then loaded onto wheelbarrows and rushed to the kiln where they were stacked into neat piles. The engine at the works ran on gas produced from anthracite. Trucks full of the coal arrived at Blisworth station and were turned by hand onto a track running down into the brickyard where they were emptied. A horse hauled the empty trucks back up to the station. It took four men to turn the big flywheel round to start the engine up and Ernie 'Bowie' Cockerill sat outside winding a handle to blow the gas through. The engine would start with a 'Chuff... Chuff... Chuff'. And once started would suck the gas through by itself.

Tom Powell, the fireman

Tom Powell, the fireman, kept the brickworks fired up for two and a half weeks at a time, so the men had to operate 24 hours a day. Tom started with a slow burn by putting slack (small coal) into little holes and leaving this to burn up. Whilst waiting, the men would pass the time drinking their favourite beer from the barrel at the Navigation Inn at Blisworth/Gayton Arm. But they worked hard and had earned their beer.

Wilson's

Wilson, the builder, built two brick houses in Back Lane before the Second World War. He lived in one and rented the other out, generally to nurses. The brickworks on Wright's Lane was opened to provide bricks for the new housing development. It closed for a while but was re-opened by the Banbury Lane Brick Company. As the works had to operate 24 hours a day a small room was provided for the men to use over night.

Bravery

By 1952 the buildings were rather dilapidated and there was a near fatal accident. Harry George fell from the roof through the chimney into the hot sand in the kiln below. Two men, Joe Billing and Ted Paul, rushed in and with no thought for their own safety, pulled him out. Without question they saved his life. The works were shut down a short time later.

Pattishall Accident Club

Many Gayton men joined the Pattishall Accident Club which gave its members an insurance in case of accident. Men joined at 14 when they started work and for Harry it proved an invaluable help. He was in hospital for 11 weeks and was 'on the Club' for 11 months.

Bombs

During the Second World War the night skies of Gayton were lit by fires from the bombing of the city of Coventry. On one occasion two bombs were dropped in the pits at the brickyard. They were probably surplus bombs aimed at the canal by one of the German planes which passed over the village on its way home.

Asplin's brickworks

On the parish border with Milton Malsor, Blisworth and Gayton, the Asplin brickworks differed from the other Gayton brickyards as they were fired from the bottom rather than the top. The bricks produced are recognisable due to the holes running through them. The two red-brick cottages opposite the Queen Victoria pub were built with Asplin's bricks. Interestingly this company was doing repair work for the church even though Evered Brown, the manager of a rival firm, was churchwarden.

Ironstone mining

Profitable mining in the 1850s
The local stone in Gayton has a high iron content. This features as an attractive honey colour which contrasts with the plain grey limestone. Although limestone is a better, longer lasting building material the local houses incorporating ironstone have a softer more appealing look.

The workings
Commercial quarrying of the Gayton stone began in 1853. The quarry owner was John Hickman but he worked in conjunction with Pell and Co., of Heyford from 1858 until they took over completely.

Ironstone workers

Left to right:
Back row   Harry Wootton, Frank Nightingale, Jack Nightingale, Aubrey Shipperley, Harry George, Tom Powell
Front row   George Scott, Arthur Wootton, Reg Nightingale, Charles Hillyer, Fred Pinnegar

At the Ironstone works where steep slopes made the ironstone working difficult

Account book for Ironstone workers in 1918

Pell and Co.

In 1858 Pell and Co., were producing 75,000 tons and J Hickman, 3,395 tons. Although the name changed to Heyford Iron and Co., in March 1874 it was probably still operated by Pell and Co. Leases were held by John Clare, John Hickman, Sir Joseph Henry Hawley and also John Butcher. A tramway connection ran between the opencast pits of Gayton and the main railway line to the north. John Deykin Clare was a mineral merchant of Yardley, Birmingham who took the ironstone from Gayton and sent it on to Staffordshire. The wages were higher for the ironstone workers than for the rural workers, making Gayton's miners relatively prosperous. The original pits were exhausted in 1883 and the operation was closed completely by 1899. However, in 1900 the quarries were re-opened by R B Sparrow of Blisworth, who worked the system until 1921, when out-cropping ironstone was practically exhausted.

Henry William Wheldon

A second operation was opened by Henry W Wheldon, a gentleman already well known on the Birmingham Exchange, who bought land in Gayton in 1863 and removed ironstone supplying the Birmingham, Staffordshire and South Wales markets where it was in demand. He operated until 1884. The site involved difficulties with loading onto the railway as the sidings were extremely steep. In 1867 Stanton Ironworks Company started to receive ore by canal from Gayton, perhaps from Wheldon. It was probably loaded at Blisworth Wharf which is nearer the mining than Gayton Wharf at Banbury Lane.

Gayton organist

Henry Wheldon had been a chorister at New College, Oxford. When he came to live at Rensbury, Baker Street, he pursued his musical interest by playing the church organ from 1870 to 1920.

The Nurse

Mrs Eykyn guaranteed the nurse's wage

Mrs Eykyn instigated an innovative scheme in 1904 to provide Gayton, Tiffield and Blisworth with a nurse. Although Tiffield opted out in 1907 they re-joined in 1919 with Rothersthorpe when Blisworth left. Mrs Eykyn guaranteed for three years Gayton's part of the nurse's salary which was £48 2s *per annum* plus a maintained bicycle. The nurse soon became greatly appreciated although inevitably people took advantage and restrictions had to be put upon her duties. She only sat up at night with a patient on an order from the Doctor or in the case of an emergency. The village was continually fundraising for the Nurses' Association. Mary Dunckley, the assistant school mistress, in 1910 left a legacy of £5 which went to the bicycle fund. In 1911 the servants at Gayton House organised a Fancy Dress Ball which took place at the school. Approximately 90 people attended and the dancing went on till 3am.

Nurse Sharpe

Nurse Sharpe was Parish Nurse for 12 years (1904-16) eventually going on to become a Health Visitor. A water bed, which had been in use for many years, required replacement and so she organised the collection. There was such a generous response that £4 8s 4d was raised which enabled her not only to purchase a new bed, but to get the old one patched up and to invest in a hot water bottle as well. Her services were greatly in demand and at a meeting of the Nursing Association on 5 June 1914 it was decided to make an extra charge for massage. Nurse Sharpe taught the village women about nursing. She held a course of talks at Mrs C Lucas' (Gogg's Farm) on a Monday evening for women and girls over 14 years old. She was an active member of the community having a particular flair for flower arranging.

Nurse Hillyer

Nurse Hillyer kept up the women's education and in 1916 she gave a talk on nursing and bandaging at a WI meeting. She was a much loved nurse but very eccentric. One story tells of the doctor arriving at her house to see patients, handing her his bowler hat and at the same time asking for boiling water. She returned with the water in his hat!

Nurses Kenny and Harlow

Nurse Kenny after her time in Gayton left for New Zealand from where she kept in touch. She wrote for many years to her Gayton friends reporting her marriage and the birth of a son. Nurse Harlow was the nurse in 1920 at the time of Revd King's death. Mr Chester and Mr Ratledge arranged a Whist Drive the proceeds of which went towards a much needed new bicycle for her.

Left to right:
Back row   unknown, Hilda Wakelin, Mrs Charlie Rook, Mrs Newcomb,
            Mrs Cokayne, Linda Evans
Front row   unknown, unknown, Nurse Edwards, Mrs Keenes

District Nurse Edwards in uniform
c1950

Nurse Edwards

Nurse Mary Ellen Edwards was Gayton's last nurse as the post was no longer required with the arrival of the National Health Service. However, when in 1947 she suffered an accident, Nurse Budden looked after the people of Gayton. Nurse Edwards worked in Gayton for more than 20 years completing her nursing career within the NHS as a District Nurse.

The Royal Mail

Early postal services

In 1849 Gayton's post was dealt with in Northampton although letters also arrived in Towcester from London, at four in the morning and at a quarter to two in the afternoon. Towcester mail was sent on to Gayton by the Post Master, Josiah Simco. He dispatched it at nine in the morning and ten at night. By 1869 letters went through Northampton which was the nearest money order office. Gayton had a wall letter box by 1874. Letters from Northampton arrived at 9am and were sent at 4.30pm. But it was not until 1876 that Gayton had a recognised postal service. This was a railway sub-office which required a railway employee to collect, every morning, the sack of mail dropped off by a train in a dangerous manoeuvre as it sped by. This could have been the job of Robert Edmunds, Harry Lawrence, Henry Clarke, Thomas Clarke, George Cockerill, William Richardson, Jesse Smith, Tom Ingle, George Inns, Frederick Hillyard or John Brandom, all of whom worked on the railway.

Joseph Ratledge

Joseph Ratledge, a stone mason by trade and still clerk of the parish at 66 years old, became Gayton's first salaried sub-postmaster in 1885. He was living in Doctor's Row and his home, today called Beech House, became Gayton's first Post Office and consequently the row of cottages built onto Beech House sometime after 1831 came to be called Post Office Row. The postal arrangements now improved and the mail came up from Blisworth Railway sub-Post Office and were received at 7.30am and sent at 4.30pm. There was no service on Sundays and the nearest money order office was at Blisworth. By 1890 an extra dispatch was included at 6.15pm and in 1894 there was an extra delivery made at 2pm.

Beech House, the first Post Office, the home of Joseph Ratledge

A Telegraph Office

In 1890, an application to upgrade the sub-Post Office at Gayton to a Telegraph Office was not thought to be commercially viable by the Post Office, but Arthur Eykyn guaranteed it with a bond. This arrangement continued for many years and was not formally rescinded until 24 July 1941.

Neglect of duty

Postman A J Gibbs broke Post Office rules by stopping off at the pub when he returned to Blisworth with the Gayton mail. He also carried a can of milk from the pub to the Railway Hotel, and returned with the empty can in the evening, all whilst on Post Office duty. The report, advocating Gibbs' dismissal, complained, 'This is the third time that Gibbs has been reported to Head Quarters for intoxication'. Nonetheless, common sense prevailed and Gibbs kept his job, although his wages were reduced from 22 shillings a week to 20. The unfortunate Joseph Ratledge was reprimanded for entrusting the mails to Gibbs whilst the latter was under the influence of drink.

A man who is not sober

On 9 April 1900 when Isabel Ratledge was about 25 years old, she became the sub-postmistress of Gayton in her father's place. At this time it is possible that the Post Office was moved to the old schoolhouse for a while. In May 1901 A J Gibbs was to get Isabel Ratledge into trouble with the authorities and cautioned like her father before her. She was informed that she must not, under any circumstances, entrust the mail to a man who was not sober. This time Gibbs, although he had been employed since 1883 and his wages were back up to 22 shillings a week, was dismissed. Four times he had been reported for intoxication and the Post Office finally lost patience with him despite Gayton residents writing to them on his behalf. The Blisworth sub-postmaster, Mr A Pike, was criticized for failing to report Gibbs on other occasions and as his record in other respects had not been satisfactory, he received a warning. Perhaps this experience explained why Isabel Ratledge walked to Blisworth and back with the mail for many years. She also delivered letters and telegrams in the village herself, before J T Miller became Gayton's postman.

Miss Isobel Ratledge

Trouble during the First World War

During the First World War, Police Constable Gardner noticed a light in the Post Office window and called Miss Ratledge's attention to it. She, no doubt, did not appreciate being reprimanded by him and refused to put up a blind as she was closing in five minutes. She was fined five shillings.

Isobel Ratledge bequeaths a Hall

Gayton showed its appreciation of Isabel Ratledge's services when she retired by making her a donation to buy a television set, but sadly she died in hospital in 1951 at 72 years old as the result of an accident, before the purchase could be made. Isabel Ratledge left the whole of her estate, which was auctioned at Beech House on Tuesday 13 March 1951 and raised £3,061 4s 9d, for a Village Hall which provides a fitting memorial to her to this day. It was opened by Mrs Hawley on 25 May 1957 and a dance was held in the evening. The Village Hall has been used as a venue for many different events over the years. In 2000 the Evergreen Club meets there regularly as does the Parish Council and Tennis Club.

At a wedding reception in the Village Hall in 1970
Left to right, Joan Keightley, Margaret Ratledge, Linda Ratledge, Barbara
Ratledge, Gladys Ratledge, Winifred Horne, Marilyn Ratledge and Terry
Ratledge

The Evergreens at the Village Hall in 1997
Left to right, Nancy Paul, Gladys Keenes, Eve Cockerill, Marion Blake and
Gladys Lucas

A change of hands

For a while following Isobel Ratledge's retirement, Mr and Mrs John East ran the Post Office
from the Well House. Soon it changed hands and was taken over by Gladys Lucas from her
home, Grey House in Baker Street. Miss Lucas was a piano teacher and broke off from the
lessons to serve customers. She also sold postcards of Gayton which can be seen on pages
86-93. Three days after she retired, 27 October 1967, the Post Office was combined with
the shop at the Queen Victoria. Later, the closure of this shop forced the Post Office to be
held in the Village Hall for two hours on a Wednesday. Ruth Woolston opened a shop from
her home in Hillcrest Road, 26 November 1979, and this enabled the Post Office to open
more frequently. When this closed in 1982 the Post Office returned once again to the
Village Hall. In the year 2000 the Post Office is being run from Mrs Ros Billing's home in
High Street.

Today's Post Office in High Street opened
on 21 November 1983

Gayton Bakehouses

Early bakers

In the middle of the nineteenth century there were two notable bakers in Gayton, William Facer at the Queen Victoria and William Rolfe at Rensbury. However Mr E Ratledge occupied a bakehouse at the Dower House for a while until it was incorporated into the main house. When William Rolfe retired, Richard Rolfe took over at first but soon passed the bakery on to Edward Linnell who worked until the late 1870s when the bakery at Rensbury closed, perhaps being taken into the house. The Queen Victoria continued as a family business with Thomas Facer the baker after William's death. Probably John Ratledge the son of the postmaster, Joseph, took over c1888 when Thomas Facer died. He was followed by John Albert Haskins the landlord of the Queen Victoria in 1914. By 1928 Richard Marston was baker at the Queen Victoria Bakehouse working through the 1930s until in 1939 Roland 'Rowey' Parish started baking Gayton's bread.

Roland Parish

When Rowey took over he improved the facilities by putting in a floor to ceiling partition to prevent draughts. John Hillyer and Bill Green did the job for 25s using materials from the first telephone box which had been at the Old Post Office at Beech House.

No cake but doughnuts!

During the first year of the war, Ray Cockerill, a school boy at Towcester Grammar School, helped Rowey by making doughnuts. They were very popular as it was not possible to buy cake.

Improvements

Mechanisation was introduced in the form of a Gilbert electric mixer which cost £50 in 1955. This could mix one sack of flour in 10-15 minutes but the kneading and moulding still had to be done by hand. In 1956 the oven was converted from coal to an oil 'Half Sack Oven'. The flue dated back to 1851 and originally burned wood faggots.

Ingredients

The flour was delivered one week by Whitworths, and by Westley Brothers and Clarke, on alternate weeks, and nine pounds of yeast was delivered every Tuesday and Friday. Larry Coles collected it in his motor bike and sidecar from the London train at Northampton station and delivered it to the bakehouse. Rowey's recipe was:

> 1 sack of Canadian flour, 3 buckets of hot water, 1¼ lbs fresh yeast, 2¼ lbs salt.
> This recipe made 212 loaves (two batches).

It was a long working day, with a 6am start and 9.30pm finish. If Rowey wanted time off he would bake until midnight the night before as the villagers depended on his delivery. On a normal day the first batch of loaves was ready for the oven at 9.30am and he would bake another batch later in the day. In the afternoon he would deliver to Gayton, Blisworth, Milton and Rothersthorpe.

William Newcomb and Richard Marston remembering at the Cenotaph

End of an era

The bakery was forced to close as Rowey could not afford the cost of the modernisation necessary for the new health regulations. The cost of a loaf had risen from 4½d in 1939 when Rowey started, to 1s 8d in 1969 when he stopped. The oven door and surrounds were reset in the Queen Victoria, the original site of the bakery, and they are still more or less in the same place.

The Evergreens' Christmas Party at the Queen Victoria, 1997,
with the Bakehouse oven in the background

Left to right:
Left table   Cyril Smith, Audrey Smith, Nancy Paul, Harry George, Leila Walsh
Right table   Sam Cockayne, Edith Cockayne, Marion Blake

Feasts, Fêtes and Fancy Dress

The National United Order of Free Gardeners

The National United Order of Free Gardeners, despite its name, had nothing whatsoever to do with gardening! It was a Friendly Society established in 1820 which enabled working men, by paying a weekly subscription, to claim money when sick and unable to work. Children could also be enrolled in the 'club'. The medical officer of the Society attended members and medicine was provided free.

Gayton's Rosebud Lodge

Gayton's branch of the Gardeners, Rosebud Lodge, number 1,161, was started in 1873. Gayton's Club Feast was essentially a male event but the whole village joined in on the Sunday and Monday following May Day. In the early years the children were given a week's holiday from school but in the 1900s this was shortened to the Monday and Tuesday.

Gardener's sash

Rosebud Lodge was part of Northampton District and Gayton's representatives attended the District's functions

May Club Feast days

Everyone gathered outside the headquarters of the Rosebud Lodge on the Sunday. This was the present school building on Bugbrooke Road but prior to 1900 had been the old schoolhouse in Deans Row. To the summons of the church bells and led by one of the local bands, for example, the Wootton Band or in 1910 the Bugbrooke Excelsior Brass Band, they 'marched' to the church in procession, with the men wearing their sashes.

Only time men went to church

An evening service was held in the church and the proceeds of the collection went to society funds. This was followed by the band playing on the triangle at Fiveways, after which the men retired to their favoured drinking establishments to celebrate. For many Gayton men their wedding day and Feast Sunday were the only times they went to church!

Club Monday

The festivities began again on the Monday when the women produced a sumptuous annual dinner for the men. Much preparation went into this meal and many of the girls were absent from school in the preceding week. Long trestle tables had to be brought from the Rectory, as did the crockery and china, which bore the inscription 'St Mary's Church'. Vegetables were cooked in large coppers, which were stored in the out-houses at the school for this occasion. The Yorkshire puddings and joints were cooked in the oven at the Queen Victoria's bakery and carried ceremoniously up the road to the school.

The men's dinner

The sashes were once again brought out from the trunks in the infants' room and the annual dinner was held in the school. The meal took all afternoon as there was much drinking of toasts and speech making. In 1898 Mr E J Brown, whilst making the toast to the Chairman, Mr George, said that it was impossible for anyone to support a cause more noble than theirs, which aimed at the common brotherhood of man and in making provision for sickness and help for their wives and families at death. By 1907 the speech making had turned to politics, demanding the Government bring in an old age pension.

Rosebud Lodge declines

Membership of Gayton's Rosebud Lodge declined over the years, and was eventually merged with the Milton Lodge. The reduction in membership of Friendly Societies was mirrored across the country due to the introduction of the Welfare State. In Gayton and Milton's case it was made worse by the scandal of the Milton Treasurer running away with their funds!

Fancy dress

At the turn of the century villagers had to make their own entertainment and fancy dress balls, parties, parades and competitions were popular. A women's club called the Welcome Club put on just such an event one Friday evening. The party consisted of about one hundred women and girls, each member having been entitled to invite two friends.

The Dairymaids' Supper

The members of the club put on a musical entertainment called *The Dairymaids' Supper* in the schoolroom. The farmer, his wife and a bevy of dairymaids, milk cans, a pump and chalk all took part. The dairymaids clad in white dresses, red belts and sunbonnets performed a milking stool drill and Swedish dance. The piece ended with a call to supper from the farmer, which was responded to by the dairymaids, cans and pump, all taking a dish from the well laden table and handing the supper around to the guests. To round off the evening Mrs Boycott and the Misses King sang *Three Little Maids from School* through a screen decorated with sunflowers. At 9.30pm the company made a ring and crossed arms and sang *Auld Lang Syne* followed by the *National Anthem*.

Georgina and Beatrice Inns dressed as Dairymaids
for a Welcome Club Revue

Ray and Margaret Newcomb, photographed c1920
in Kiln Yard where they lived

The Payne family wholeheartedly joined in the fun of dressing up

John and Bertha Payne in costume for a New Year Party

Royal holidays

Edward VII's Coronation, 1902

In the last century the village celebrated the sovereign's coronation as a community. For weeks they all subscribed to a fund which enabled them to provide free food and fun. In 1902 the money was spent on producing a free dinner.

George V's Coronation, 1911

A free dinner and tea was held in 1911 to celebrate George V's coronation. The festivities in Gayton commenced at 6am with a 'merry' peal of bells. At 10.30am the schoolchildren, the teachers, managers and friends met to salute the flag. After singing the *National Anthem* and a short speech given by the Rector, a procession was formed and they all marched to the church for a short service. Mrs King presented every child with a coronation mug. Dinner was held at noon for those over 65, but with the children being served first. Mr G H Dunckley of Evergreen Farm lent a field for sports in the afternoon. Tea was at 5pm and the prizes were presented by Miss Cecile Eykyn. Dancing until midnight in the schoolroom concluded the day.

Royal marriages

At 9am on 10 March 1863 King Edward and Queen Alexandra were married. So were Mr and Mrs Clarke and Mr and Mrs Ben Smith. The day was a public holiday. The wedding service at Gayton church was performed by the curate, Revd Whitehurst. The weather was 'very foggy and proper cold' according to Mr Clarke. Their wedding breakfast was held at Banbury Lane. Afterwards the two young couples joined the rest of the village in the celebrations for the royal wedding held on Walter George's field. Mr Smith and Mrs Clarke were brother and sister and Mrs Smith had come to Gayton to work at Gayton House for Charles Pilgrim. Fifty years later on 10 March 1913 the couples celebrated their joint golden wedding. Both couples had lived all their married life in Gayton. The village joined in their celebrations by ringing a peal of bells in their honour in the evening.

A Village Celebration in the 1930s. In the foreground is William Newcomb and directly behind him, Freddie Hefford. The man with the beard is not known but the woman is Mrs Moore and the girl, Olive Folwell.

Celebrating George VI's Coronation

George VI's Coronation, 1937
George VI's coronation was commemorated in 1937 by a free tea and sports and the WI planted a silver birch on the village green.

Elizabeth II's Coronation, 1953
This was celebrated with a free tea and mug for the children. The elderly people of Gayton went on a coach trip to see the local decorations.

After the Second World War

Dick Barton, Special Agent
The British Legion Fete on 3 July 1948 was one of the first events to take place after the war. It was held at the Old Rectory (now Wendover) and organised by Mr Garnham who was living at Fiveways. It was an extremely successful event, fondly remembered especially as it was opened by radio's 'Dick Barton'. One story that contributed to the radio actor's popularity was that the Gayton British Legion Treasurer, William Rowe, gave Noel Johnson (Dick Barton) £25 to spend at the fete so that he could go around and talk to the stall holders. At the end of the afternoon, after having spent freely at each stall, he returned the £25 to the Treasurer. It was a much appreciated gesture.

In 1948 the British Legion invited the hugely popular Noel Johnson, or Dick Barton, Special Agent as he was better known, to open the Fête. It proved a great success.

Gayton joins the Merry Comrades
Auntie Dick (Mrs E E Field) wrote a children's page for the *Mercury and Herald* newspaper. By writing to the newspaper children could join the Merry Comrades. On their birthdays the children had their names printed in the newspaper. It was necessary to have raised money for a variety of good causes to be included on the Merry Comrades Day Out. The Gayton leaders were Mrs Keenes and Miss Nellie Cockerill, who was housekeeper to Revd Browne. In 1949 Gayton raised £20 for the Hospitals Radio and Comforts Fund and in 1952 a party of Gayton's Merry Comrades attended a presentation where the youngest comrade, Angela Hillyer, presented Auntie Dick with £10 raised by a dance. The boys at Gayton School were

taught to knit squares in one plain, one purl which the girls sewed into blankets for the war effort. Perfumed 'congratulation' or 'happy birthday' cards, were sold to raise money by the Merry Comrades.

Coach outings were popular in the 1950s

Group of Merry Comrades

Left to right:

Back row   Nellie Cockerill, Edie Cockerill, Gladys Keenes, Mrs Ted Cockerill

Second row   Doris White, Sylvia Smith, Joan Paul, Shirley West, Christine Barker, Elizabeth Cockerill, Wendy Morgan, Pearl Billing, Marion Barker

Third row   Pat East, Ann Munton, Jennifer Nightingale, Beryl Keenes, Joyce Munton, Daphne Hillyard, Kate Carney, Ruth Cockerill

Front row   Yvonne Donnay, Diana Billing, Gill Donnay, Christine Cockerill, Vivienne Carney, Madeline Bevan, Kay Goosey

Women's Institute

The Women's Institute was formed on 20 September 1918. The first committee under the President Mrs George King and Secretary, Mrs Meredith, was Mrs William George, Miss Wootton, Miss King, Mrs Ratledge, Mrs Moore, Mrs Frost, Mrs Roughton, Mrs Puxley, Mrs Payne and Miss A Hillyer. Soon there were 60 members. The Institute disbanded during the Second World War from 1940-45. When it re-opened with Miss Parr from Corner Cottage as President, it soon flourished. Miss Parr was involved with amateur dramatics and the post-war years were notable for the productions either undertaken by Gayton WI or with them contributing. In 1953 the President was Mrs Major-Lucas, Secretary Mrs Berridge, with committee members, Mrs Buttolph, Mrs Chester, Mrs Folwell, Mrs Hildred, Mrs Marston, Mrs Morgan, Mrs Rogers, Mrs Ratledge, Mrs Thomas, Mrs Thursfield and Mrs Tattersall. In 1992, deciding that Gayton women at this time had too many commitments and being unable to raise a committee, Gayton WI reluctantly took the decision to close. It has been missed.

Gayton Women's Institute 1972

Left to right:
Back row   Thelma Parish, Gladys Green, Janet Wilkins, Gwen Crossley, Win Maycock, Wendy Briglin, Barbara Hillyard, a lady from Tiffield, Iris Robinson, Barbara Wilkins, Mrs Mayes, Mrs Brown
Middle row   Mrs Rook, Viv Carney, Mrs Hulbert, Sandra Pennock, Hazel Harris, Miss Boyes, Mrs Buckley, Miss Boyes, Mrs Goodyer, Miss Eyden
Front row   Mrs Baker, Mrs Rogers, Gwen Brown, Joan Chester, Miss Lucas, Mrs Ivy Morgan, Mrs Thomas and Mrs Major-Lucas

The WI preparing for a performance of *The Little White Bull*
Left to right:
Back row   Edie Reeve, Ada Rogers, Valerie Penn, Barbara Bryan, Pat Rogers, Iris Robinson, Beryl Markham
Front row   Ruth Cockerill

Gayton Mothers' Union
Left to right:
Back row   Marion Butcher, Mrs Thomas, Mrs Major Lucas, Olive Morgan, Mrs Wright, Gladys Keenes, Linda Kingston, Mrs N Paul, Mrs Bull, Mrs Boot, Mrs Wilkins snr, Mrs Mansfield, Mrs A Webb
Middle row   Sarah Anne Hillyard (in chair), Mrs White, Mrs J East, Mrs Paul snr, Mrs Folwell, Mrs Marsden, Mrs Bridget Smith, Mrs Georgina Hillyer
Front row   Olive Billing, Gladys White, Mrs Hildred, Mrs Johns, Mrs Roe, Mrs George, Mrs Ted Cockerill, Rita Hillyer with Angela, Thelma Mansfield and Mrs Bull's daughter, Pam Mansfield and Nicholas

May Day

Gayton's May time celebrations were re-started but they took a different form after the war under the auspices of the Women's Institute. Elizabeth Cockerill was crowned May Queen, on 16 May 1952 by Miss Agnes Stops who had been a leading light in the Women's Institute and the inspiration behind a tree planting campaign in Northamptonshire. The May Queen's attendants were Blodwen Bevan, Anne Donnay, Jane Kingston and Valerie Reid. The celebrations took place in the Manor House grounds as they did in 1953 when Beryl Keenes was May Queen. The best garland prize winners were Michael Cockerill, Frances Bevan, Terry Webb, John Webster, Hazel Shipperley, Ian Goodridge, Madeline Bevan, Graham Reid, Ann Munton and Christine Cockerill. Tea was served at the school. The May Queen and her attendants led a parade of people around the village, ending at the village green.

In 1972 Rachel East was May Queen
Left to right: Karl and Kevin Hillyard, Sharon Hiscoke at the back, Kathleen Ratledge, Sarah East, Jane Ratledge and May Queen, Rachel East, with Adrian Briglin standing watching the proceedings

Avis Bevan, May Queen with her attendants in 1966
Left to right: boy, Barbara Cokayne, Kay Goosey, Ann Parish, Avis Bevan, Jennifer Wilkins, Jackie Smith, Stuart Woolston and David Wilkins

Gemma Clinch, the May Queen in 1992, rode in style in a carriage provided by Pam and Roger Clayton

Sarah James the May Queen in 1993, riding Shariff led by Rachel Billing, with attendants and Alison Foster following, leading the village parade

The early May Day celebrations took place in
the manor-house grounds

May Day 1954 with Ann Munton as May Queen. The soldiers'
costumes were popular with the boys and used for several years.

In 1956 when Chris Cockerill was May Queen, the Old Manor
Farm could be seen from the school grounds as the Bugbrooke
Road had yet to be developed

Maypole Dancing in 1993 supervised by Head Teacher Mrs North

May Day Parade 1961

May Queen in 1974, Claire Newcomb, was crowned by Mrs Goodridge who later became Mrs Lou Thomas

Jubilee Celebrations 1977

Mrs Elizabeth Blundell (née Cockerill), Gayton's first May Queen, returned in 1977 to crown the Jubilee Queen, Sharon Hiscoke. The attendants in 1977 were Dawn Etherington, Elianne Simms, Elizabeth Mayes, Jonathan Agar and Philip Steer.

May Day Sports for the children

Left to right: front row of boys running, Brian Parish, Stuart Wilkins, Martin Bryan, Norman Cokayne, unknown, Michael Munns, John Rogers.
Behind the runners, three unknown girls, Ken Cokayne, Merryn Robinson, David Wilkins, and an unknown baby.

Playing the Game

Because of difficulties of travel and communications, all villages have had to look to themselves to provide their own sport and entertainment. Gayton has been no exception, with a variety of activities being organised at different times.

The Football Team

In 1907 a football club was started. Mr F C George was Chairman, J C George was Captain and Ernest Dunckley, Secretary. The football field was off the Milton Road just beyond the Churchyard where the bungalows are now built.

Gayton Football Team 1911

The man in the dark suit on the left is thought to be a 'Nightingale' from Blisworth, and the man in the white jacket on the right Teddy Johnson. On the back row in the dark jumper is Bert Cockerill and next to him in the white shirt is Walt Hillyer. Jack George, a Gayton farmer, is in the middle of the picture and next to him Frank Wakelin's brother.

Gayton Cricket Club

Gayton Cricket Club was first formed in 1892 but little information is available about the early days. Home games were played in the field behind the old Rectory (Wendover) and later in the field next to Outback on Back Lane. The most famous pre-war match is the one that was played against Sir David Hawley's Cambridge University Team in 1931 when, contrary to expectations, Gayton won!

Gayton Cricket Club 1931 v Cambridge University XI

Left to right:

Back row   six unkown men, Charlie Rook (Secretary), D Cockerill (Captain), W Woolacot, Mr Crask (President), F Chester and Reg Parish

Front row   three unknown men, Sir David Hawley (wearing a cravat and jacket), G Mesham, H Hillyard, W Garrett, F Eales and D Hicks

The tea makers c1953

Left to right:

Back row: Eric White, Vera George, Gladys White, Brian Ratledge, Marion Butcher

Front row   May Carney, Friend of Mrs Carney, Mrs Barker, Edie Cockerill, Ted Gould

Gayton Cricket Club c1954

Left to right:
Back row   Ken Cokayne, Mr Cokayne, Bruce Peck, Mr Goddard, Don Reekie (landlord of the Eykyn Arms, George Clark, Luke Freeman

Middle row   Michael Essery, Denis Cockerill, Mrs Thomas, Bernard Mansfield, Ray Newcomb

Front row   Gerald Morgan, Cyril Smith, Walter Newcomb, Reg Parish

Gayton Ladies' Cricket Team who played the men's Cricket Team in July 1981

Left to right:
Back row   Kathleen Bobsin, Jean Ratledge, Rosemarie Bryan, Chris Carter, Sonia Church, Rachel East, Ann North, Julie Bryan

Middle row Penny Miles, Jane Dexter, Ann Summerbell, Sharon Hiscoke with Angela Roberts in front

After the second World War the club re-formed and played its home games at the old cricket field at Blisworth Road/Back Lane. There are fond memories of four Gayton cricketers. Walt Newcomb was the Club's longest serving Secretary and scorer for 20 years. Bernard Mansfield, a great Club man before his death at a far too early age, was an inspiration to young players. Neil Bobsin, was the Club's greatest wicket taker ever. And finally, 'Nobby' George, umpire known for his, 'There's no ifs, buts or maybes about it, mate. You're out'. In 2000, the home ground is at Westgate House in Eastcote Road, where a new pavilion has been built and Merryn Robinson is the custodian of the Club's records.

Gayton Golf Club

In 1907 the Rector, the doctor and a few other notables from the village had an afternoon playing golf on the newly opened links on William George's land on the righthand side of Wright's Lane. Mr Boycott from Outback was in charge of tending to the course. Almost a century later, Gayton's golfing tradition is maintained in the form of the Eykyn Stags Golf Society, whose members play each other on a regular basis.

Eykyn Arms Skittle Team

Ted Paul and his team from the Eykyn Arms played in the Gayton and District Skittles Championship, winning the Trophy in 1967. When Ted Paul died in 1977, Mac Woolston, a skilled wood carver, produced a skittle board as a memorial trophy to Ted. To stand alongside the skittle board, he carved a model of Ted Paul out of a skittle. The winner of the trophy, although awarded the skittle board, was presented with a cup to keep, whilst the board itself remained in the Eykyn Arms public house, where it can be seen today in the front window.

Ted Paul Memorial Trophy
Left to right, Laurie Adams, Mac Woolston, Joan Adams and Paul Adams

Darts Teams

Queen Victoria Darts Presentation at the Salon, St James, Northampton, in 1960

Left to right:

Back row   Denis Smith, Jack Sheppard

Third row   Reg Parrish, Denis Cockerill, Reg Green (behind Joe Billing), Bill Reid, Bob (Ted) Mansfield (behind Ray Newcomb), Bernard Mansfield, Mervyn Cockerill, Gerald Fowler, Bill Jacobs, Herbert Stewart

Second row   Ron Webb, Joe Billing, Ray Newcomb, Paul Kirtchmere

Front row   Harry George, Gerald Collins (landlord of the Queen Victoria), Walter Newcomb, John Hillyer

Eykyn Arms Darts Team 1953

Left to right:

Back row   Ray Newcomb, Cyril Smith, Denis Cockerill, Bernard Mansfield, Walt Newcomb

Front row   Arthur, Bill Reid, Bob Mansfield, Reg Green, Cliff Crossley (landlord of the Eykyn Arms)

Darts was a popular village sport when Cliff Cossley was landlord of the Eykyn Arms. Later, the Queen Victoria Darts Team was formed when Gerald Collins, himself an excellent player, became the landlord there. They were very successful in the Phipps' Darts League in Northampton in the late 1950s, eventually reaching the premier section.

Rural sports

Thomas Payne c1910 who was landlord of the Red Lion and a farmer who evidently also enjoyed rural sports

Clay Shooting, Street Fair July 1991
Richard Huckerby trying to teach Rita Poxon to hit the clay!

Sledging at Springs Orchard
For as long as can be remembered Springs Orchard has been the venue for Gayton children to enjoy this popular winter past-time

Index of People

Index of Places